S. Hrg. 114–236

CONFRONTING THE CHALLENGE OF CYBERSECURITY

FIELD HEARING

BEFORE THE

COMMITTEE ON COMMERCE, SCIENCE, AND TRANSPORTATION UNITED STATES SENATE

ONE HUNDRED FOURTEENTH CONGRESS

FIRST SESSION

SEPTEMBER 3, 2015

Printed for the use of the Committee on Commerce, Science, and Transportation

U.S. GOVERNMENT PUBLISHING OFFICE

99–806 PDF   WASHINGTON : 2016

For sale by the Superintendent of Documents, U.S. Government Publishing Office
Internet: bookstore.gpo.gov   Phone: toll free (866) 512–1800; DC area (202) 512–1800
Fax: (202) 512–2104   Mail: Stop IDCC, Washington, DC 20402–0001

SENATE COMMITTEE ON COMMERCE, SCIENCE, AND TRANSPORTATION

ONE HUNDRED FOURTEENTH CONGRESS

FIRST SESSION

JOHN THUNE, South Dakota, *Chairman*

ROGER F. WICKER, Mississippi
ROY BLUNT, Missouri
MARCO RUBIO, Florida
KELLY AYOTTE, New Hampshire
TED CRUZ, Texas
DEB FISCHER, Nebraska
JERRY MORAN, Kansas
DAN SULLIVAN, Alaska
RON JOHNSON, Wisconsin
DEAN HELLER, Nevada
CORY GARDNER, Colorado
STEVE DAINES, Montana

BILL NELSON, Florida, *Ranking*
MARIA CANTWELL, Washington
CLAIRE McCASKILL, Missouri
AMY KLOBUCHAR, Minnesota
RICHARD BLUMENTHAL, Connecticut
BRIAN SCHATZ, Hawaii
EDWARD MARKEY, Massachusetts
CORY BOOKER, New Jersey
TOM UDALL, New Mexico
JOE MANCHIN III, West Virginia
GARY PETERS, Michigan

DAVID SCHWIETERT, *Staff Director*
NICK ROSSI, *Deputy Staff Director*
REBECCA SEIDEL, *General Counsel*
JASON VAN BEEK, *Deputy General Counsel*
KIM LIPSKY, *Democratic Staff Director*
CHRIS DAY, *Democratic Deputy Staff Director*
CLINT ODOM, *Democratic General Counsel and Policy Director*

(II)

CONTENTS

CONFRONTING THE CHALLENGE OF CYBERSECURITY

THURSDAY, SEPTEMBER 3, 2015

U.S. SENATE,
COMMITTEE ON COMMERCE, SCIENCE, AND TRANSPORTATION,
Madison, SD.

The Committee met, pursuant to notice, at 2:30 p.m., in room 203, Tunheim Classroom Building, Dakota State University, Madison, South Dakota, Hon. John Thune, Chairman of the Committee, presiding.

Present: Senator Thune [presiding].

OPENING STATEMENT OF HON. JOHN THUNE,
U.S. SENATOR FROM SOUTH DAKOTA

The CHAIRMAN. Good afternoon, everybody. I will call this Senate Commerce Committee field hearing to order and welcome you all today. We are going to talk about the challenges of cyberspace. And I am proud to bring this hearing to Dakota State University, which is nationally recognized for its cybersecurity programs.

I am also pleased to see so many DSU students here today as we discuss this important issue. Many of you students who are in the audience today are the next generation of cyber professionals that we will need to protect our private businesses and government networks from cyber incidents and attacks.

A number of you participate in the National Science Foundation's CyberCorps Scholarship for Service program, which helps increase the cybersecurity workforce at government agencies.

Federal agencies need help, especially when it comes to improving their own cybersecurity practices. You may have read in the news about cyber attacks this year on unclassified e-mail networks at the Pentagon, the State Department, and even the White House.

If any of you have ever applied for a security clearance, which some of you probably do in conjunction with the CyberCorps job application process, then you have probably been subject to the breach of background investigation information at the Office of Personnel Management. Similar compromises of sensitive information occurred with the Internal Revenue Service this year.

While these cybersecurity attacks and breaches are a problem for Federal agencies in Washington, D.C., cyber threats are important to South Dakotans, as well. The same state-sponsored hackers and criminal groups that are attacking the Federal Government to gain access to sensitive or classified information are using similar techniques to steal intellectual property from our businesses and critical infrastructure, disrupt and deny access to our online services,

(1)

and steal our identities and personal information to fraudulently spend money in our names.

Two weeks ago, I spoke to Sioux Falls residents at a Stop, Think, Connect event hosted by the National Cyber Security Alliance to educate consumers and local businesses about how to add security layers to their everyday online activities. Good Internet practices like creating strong passwords, recognizing phishing e-mails, and two-factor authentication go a long way toward helping protect yourself online.

We likely won't ever find one silver bullet solution or set of solutions to cybersecurity vulnerabilities, but we can continue to improve our ability to manage and mitigate cyber risks.

Congress has a role in this effort, and the Senate plans to consider legislation, the Cybersecurity Information Sharing Act of 2015, that would spur greater cyber threat information-sharing between and among the private sector and the government. The addition of liability protections under the bill would allow businesses to share information more easily across industry sectors or among groups of companies that may be experiencing the same cyber threats.

Another bill that I believe will help address cybersecurity challenges is the Cybersecurity Enhancement Act of 2014, which I cosponsored and which passed out of the Commerce Committee and became law last year.

This law included important provisions for R&D, workforce development, and standards. It authorized the National Institute of Standards and Technology's continued efforts to develop the voluntary framework for critical infrastructure cybersecurity, the National Science Foundation's successful CyberCorps scholarship program, and NIST's National Initiative for Cybersecurity Education, known as NICE.

It also directed better cooperation and planning across Federal agencies in research and development and updated efforts on cloud computing and international standards.

I believe these legislative efforts are a significant step forward, but I hope that we can spend some time today discussing future efforts to address the ongoing cybersecurity challenge, including the importance of honing our ability to conduct offensive cyber operations when appropriate.

I want to thank all of our witnesses for agreeing to testify today, and I am grateful to Dakota State University for hosting this hearing.

I want to express my appreciation to Dr. Josh Pauli, a DSU professor and one of our witnesses today, for helping to arrange this hearing and being an excellent host to the other witnesses. I am always proud to tell my colleagues about DSU's prestigious designations in cybersecurity from the National Security Agency.

Also joining us from DSU is Dr. Kevin Streff, who chairs the Cybersecurity Operations and Security Department and founded his own business based on his research at DSU. His company, Secure Banking Solutions, aims to improve security at community banks here in South Dakota and across the country.

Joining us from Sioux Falls are Mark Shlanta and Mr. Eric Pulse, who represent local companies that deal with managing cyber threats as part of their businesses. Mark Shlanta's company, SDN Communications, responds to numerous daily threats against its network and customers. And at Eide Bailly, Eric Pulse advises healthcare, insurance, and financial services companies on IT risks and regulatory compliance and often looks to NIST standards as part of this effort.

I look forward to hearing from both of you and, in particular, learning about your experience with the NIST framework.

I would also like to offer a special thanks to Mr. Jeremy Epstein from NSF and Mr. Kevin Stine from NIST, who flew all the way from Washington, D.C., to testify. NSF and NIST, which are agencies under the Commerce Committee's jurisdiction, support important work in cybersecurity research, education, awareness, and standards that we will hear more about today.

Mr. Epstein is responsible for NSF's cybersecurity research program, which spans many different disciplines. Mr. Stine will discuss NIST's extensive cybersecurity work with the private sector, with other agencies, and academic institutions.

NIST has been an important partner in helping protect the nation's technology infrastructure through efforts like its successful collaboration with industry to develop the Cybersecurity Framework and technology solutions at the National Cybersecurity Center of Excellence.

So, gentlemen, I want to thank you all for being here today and look forward to hearing your testimony.

As I mentioned, I am going to provide an order here, and we will do this based on who came the farthest to come to the hearing today.

[Laughter.]

The CHAIRMAN. So we will get our two gentlemen from Washington, D.C., here to speak first.

But I want to start with Mr. Epstein, who is the Lead Program Director, as I mentioned, of the Secure and Trustworthy Cyberspace program at the National Science Foundation; followed by Mr. Kevin Stine, Manager, Security Outreach and Integration Group, Computer Security Division, Information Technology Laboratory at the National Institute of Standards and Technology.

Try and put that on a business card, guys.

[Laughter.]

The CHAIRMAN. So we will start off with them. And then I am going to turn to Mr. Mark Shlanta, the CEO the SDN Communications, who I mentioned earlier, followed by Mr. Eric Pulse, who is the Principal Director of Risk Advisory Services at Eide Bailly.

And then we will go to Dr. Kevin Streff, Department Chair, Cyber Operations and Security, at Dakota State University and also, as I mentioned, Founder and Managing Partner of Secure Banking Solutions; and then our host today, Dr. Pauli, Professor of Cybersecurity and NSF SFS CyberCorps Program Director at Dakota State University.

So there were a lot of acronyms in that, but I am delighted to be back here at Dakota State University, and I am very proud of the work that is done by our professors here, our administration, our students. And it really is a great story. And it is a great story

4

to be able to tell to my colleagues in the Senate and other places I travel, about the work that is going on here.

And I should say, too, the guy who does our IT work in my Senate office is a graduate of Dakota State University. Nic Budde is someone who went through this fine program here and does a great job of making sure that all the trains are running on time in our office, so to speak, because we have on any given day lots of IT challenges.

But I don't think there is a bigger challenge in front of us as a country right now, with the inevitable proliferation of devices, than the issue of cybersecurity. Because over the course of the next 5 years we are going to go from 10 billion connected devices to 50 billion connected devices.

And all of you already today probably have phones or TVs or laptops, iPads, whatever, that are connected. That is only going to proliferate over the course of the next 5 years when literally everything that we do in life in the Internet of Things requires a level of connectivity. And, of course, with that comes great benefit, also risk. And that is what we are going to talk a little bit about today.

So, again, I am delighted to be able to be here and to bring the Commerce Committee to Madison, South Dakota, to the campus of Dakota State University, and wish you all the best of success in the year ahead as well as in the football game on Saturday.

[Laughter.]

The CHAIRMAN. So we are going to start, kick it off, as I said, with Mr. Epstein.

So please proceed with your remarks.

Mr. EPSTEIN. Thank you.

The CHAIRMAN. And we will try and confine it as best we can, I indicated to our panelists, to 5 minutes, and then we will open it up to some questions.

STATEMENT OF JEREMY EPSTEIN, LEAD PROGRAM DIRECTOR, SECURE AND TRUSTWORTHY CYBERSPACE (SaTC), NATIONAL SCIENCE FOUNDATION

Mr. EPSTEIN. Great. Thank you.

Good afternoon, Senator Thune and members of the Dakota State University community. It is a particular pleasure to be here. I went to college in a small town, at a university very much like this, New Mexico Tech in Socorro, New Mexico, a town of 8,000 people, a student body of 1,100. "Small colleges need love, too" was our slogan back when I went to school.

[Laughter.]

Mr. EPSTEIN. So I am Jeremy Epstein. I am the National Science Foundation's lead program officer for the Secure and Trustworthy Cyberspace program—and speaking of acronyms—within the CISE Directorate, or the Directorate of Computer and Information Science and Engineering.

As you know, NSF supports fundamental research in all disciplines, advances the progress of science and engineering, and educates the next generation of innovative leaders. I welcome this opportunity to highlight NSF's investments in cybersecurity research and education.

NSF is uniquely positioned to address both today's cyber challenges as well as the threats of the future because NSF invests in discoveries as well as the discoverers who enable fundamental scientific advances and technologies.

With the rapid pace of technological advancement, we are witnessing the tight integration of financial, business, manufacturing, and telecommunications systems into a networked, global society. These interdependencies can lead to vulnerabilities and threats, as the senator said, that challenge the security, reliability, and overall trustworthiness of critical infrastructure.

The result is a dramatic shift in the size, complexity, and diversity of cyber attacks. Indeed, today, we are witnessing attacks on cars, online merchants, healthcare providers, and, of course, the government.

NSF has long supported fundamental cybersecurity research critical to achieving a secure and trustworthy cyberspace. NSF continuously brings the problem-solving capabilities of the Nation's best minds to bear on these evolving challenges by establishing a science of cybersecurity, promoting connections between academia and industry, transitioning research into practice, and bolstering cybersecurity education and training.

In Fiscal Year 2014, NSF invested $158 million in cybersecurity research and education, including $126 million in the cross-cutting Secure and Trustworthy Cyberspace program, which I lead, which funds both research and education activities.

Research projects range from security at a foundational level, including detecting whether a silicon chip contains a malicious circuit or developing new cryptographic solutions, to the systems level, including determining strategies for securing the electrical power grid and protecting individual privacy.

Cybersecurity projects are increasingly interdisciplinary, spanning computer science, mathematics, economics, behavioral science, and education. They seek to understand, predict, and explain prevention, attack, and defense behaviors and contribute to developing strategies for remediation while preserving privacy and promoting usability.

The SaTC program, as we call it, considers these perspectives within the multidimensional cybersecurity problem space while aiming to address the challenge of moving from research to capability. Projects include center-scale activities representing far-reaching explorations motivated by deep scientific questions and grand-challenge problems in, for example, privacy, encryption, cloud, and healthcare systems.

NSF also invests in the IUCRC program—there is another acronym for you—Industry University Cooperative Research Centers, that feature high-quality, industrially relevant, fundamental research, enabling direct transfer of university-developed ideas to U.S. industry, improving its competitiveness globally. In recent years, we have seen research outcomes lead to new products and services and to numerous startups in the IT sector, bringing innovative solutions to the marketplace.

To promote this type of innovation and to ensure a well-prepared work force, cybersecurity education is critically important. The shortage of cybersecurity experts has been widely estimated in the tens or hundreds of thousands of people over the next decade.

So you all are going to be employed when you graduate.

NSF's Directorate for Computer and Information Science and Engineering, along with the Directorate for Education and Human Resources, seeks to recruit and train the next generation of cybersecurity professionals through the CyberCorps: Scholarship for Service program, which many of you participate in. This program provides tuition to U.S. citizens majoring in collegiate cybersecurity programs in exchange for government service following graduation.

To date, the Scholarship for Service program has provided scholarships to more than 2,400 students and graduated more than 1,700. CyberCorps scholarship recipients have been placed in internships and full-time positions in over 140 Federal, state, local, and tribal government agencies.

As you know, Dakota State has won two of these awards for Scholarship for Service, and a new cohort of students is anticipated, or, actually, is beginning right now.

To conclude, my testimony today has emphasized that our nation must continue to invest in long-term fundamental and game-changing research in order to match the pace and scope of today's cyber threats. NSF's interdisciplinary research and education portfolios are contributing to a next generation workforce that is increasingly cyber-aware, armed with the knowledge that it needs to protect against cyber attacks.

With robust, sustained support for foundational and multidisciplinary cybersecurity R&D, as well as partnerships such as those on display here at Dakota State, NSF contributes to the protection of our national security and the enhancement of our economic prosperity.

Thank you for the opportunity to be here, and I will turn it over to the Senator. Thank you.

[The prepared statement of Mr. Epstein follows:]

PREPARED STATEMENT OF JEREMY EPSTEIN, LEAD PROGRAM DIRECTOR, SECURE AND TRUSTWORTHY CYBERSPACE (SATC), NATIONAL SCIENCE FOUNDATION

Good afternoon, Chairman Thune, and members of the Committee. My name is Jeremy Epstein and I am the National Science Foundation (NSF) Lead Program Director for the Secure and Trustworthy Cyberspace (SaTC) program within the Computer and Information Science and Engineering (CISE) Directorate.

NSF's mission is "to promote the progress of science; to advance the national health, prosperity, and welfare; [and] to secure the national defense . . .". NSF's goals—discovery, learning, research infrastructure and stewardship—provide an integrated strategy to advance the frontiers of knowledge, cultivate a world-class, broadly inclusive science and engineering workforce, build the Nation's research capability through investments in advanced instrumentation and facilities, and support excellence in science and engineering research and education. I welcome this opportunity to highlight NSF's investments in cybersecurity research and education.

The Cybersecurity Challenge

While the advances in cybersecurity research and development (R&D) are many, the Nation must continue its investments in game-changing research if our cyber systems are to be trustworthy now and in the future. As you know, every day, we learn about more sophisticated and dangerous attacks. Why is the cybersecurity challenge so hard? In general, it's hard because attacks and defenses evolve together: a system that was secure yesterday might no longer be secure tomorrow.

NSF is uniquely positioned to address both today's cyber challenges as well as the threats of the future, because NSF invests in discoveries, as well as the discoverers who enable fundamental scientific advances and technologies.

Cyber Security Research Programs

NSF funds a broad range of activities to advance cybersecurity research, develop a well-educated and capable workforce, and to keep all citizens informed and aware. A major NSF activity is the SaTC program, led by CISE in partnership with the Directorates for Education and Human Resources (EHR), Engineering (ENG), Mathematical and Physical Sciences (MPS), and Social, Behavioral, and Economic Sciences (SBE), and funded at $126 million in FY 2015. Currently, there are over 670 active Secure and Trustworthy Cyberspace awards.

NSF's SaTC program builds on predecessor programs begun in 2002 and seeks to secure the Nation's cyberspace by addressing four perspectives within the multi-dimensional cybersecurity problem space:

- *Trustworthy computing systems,* with goals to provide the basis for designing, building, and operating a cyberinfrastructure with improved resistance and improved resilience to attack that can be tailored to meet a wide range of technical and policy requirements, including both privacy and accountability.

- *Social, behavioral and economic sciences,* with goals to understand, predict, and explain prevention, attack and/or defense behaviors and contribute to developing strategies for remediation.

- *Cybersecurity education,* with goals to promote innovation, development, and assessment of new learning opportunities and to help prepare and sustain an unrivaled cybersecurity workforce capable of developing secure cyberinfrastructure components and systems, as well as to raise the awareness of cybersecurity challenges to a more general population.

- *Secure, Trustworthy, Assured and Resilient Semiconductors and Systems (STARSS),* with goals to develop strategies, techniques, and tools that avoid and mitigate hardware vulnerabilities and lead to semiconductors and systems that are resistant and resilient to attack or tampering. STARSS is a joint effort of NSF and the Semiconductor Research Corporation (SRC), a consortium of leading technology companies.

The SaTC program further aims to address the challenge of moving from research to capability. The program supports research activities whose outcomes are capable of being implemented, applied, experimentally used, or deployed in an operational environment. Areas of emphasis for these "transition to practice" investments have included malware detection and prevention, situational understanding, data assurance, risk analysis, and software assurance.

For example, NSF-funded researchers have demonstrated the ability to remotely take over automotive control systems.[1] The researchers found that, because many of today's cars contain cellular connections and Bluetooth wireless technology, it is possible for a hacker working from a remote location to take control of various features—like the car locks and brakes—as well as to track the vehicle's location, eavesdrop on its passenger cabin, and steal vehicle data. The researchers are now working with the automotive industry to develop new methods for assuring the safety and security of on-board electronics. Both the Society for Automotive Engineers and the United States Council for Automotive Research have partnered with the researchers to initiate efforts focused on automotive security research.[2] Automotive manufacturers have also started dedicating significant resources to security.[3]

NSF-funded researchers supported by the SaTC program use testbeds such as the Cyber Defense Technology Experimental Research (DETER) Network, originally developed with NSF funding and now supported by the Department of Homeland Security (DHS) and the Remotely Accessible Virtualized Environment (RAVE) Lab, which was also developed with NSF funding and is specifically focused on cybersecurity education. As directed by *The Cybersecurity Enhancement Act of 2014,* NSF is working to identify what other testbeds are needed for cybersecurity research in the future. NSF appreciates the Committee's awareness of the national need for robust cybersecurity testbeds.

---

[1] *http://www.nytimes.com/2011/03/10/business/10hack.html*
[2] *http://www.autosec.org/faq.html*
[3] *http://www.caranddriver.com/features/can-your-car-be-hacked-feature*

Cybersecurity Education and Training Programs

The NSF Directorate for Education and Human Resources seeks to develop a well-prepared cybersecurity workforce of the future in large part through the CyberCorps®: Scholarship for Service (SFS) program.

SFS was created as a result of a May 1998 Presidential Decision Directive, which described a strategy for cooperative efforts by the government and the private sector to protect physical and cyber-based systems. In January 2000, a Presidential Executive Order defined the National Plan for Information Systems Protection, which included the Federal Cyber Services (FCS) training and education initiative and the creation of a SFS program. *The Cybersecurity Enhancement Act of 2014* directs NSF, in coordination with the U.S. Office of Personnel Management (OPM) and DHS, to continue the SFS program to recruit and train the next generation of information technology professionals, industrial control system security professionals, and security managers to meet the needs of the cybersecurity mission for federal, state, local, and tribal governments. We recognize the Chairman and the Committee's work on this legislation and appreciate the strong support for the SFS program.

The SFS program funds institutions of higher education to support undergraduate and graduate students in academic programs in cybersecurity. The students must be U.S. citizens or lawful permanent residents of the U.S., and must be able to meet the eligibility and selection criteria for government employment. Students can be supported on scholarships for up to three years, and in return, they agree to take government cybersecurity positions for the same duration as their scholarships. The government agencies eligible for job placement include federal, state, local, or tribal governments. To assist both the agencies and the students in good matches, NSF partners with OPM to run an annual job fair. In addition to OPM, NSF also partners with DHS and the National Security Agency (NSA) on the SFS program.

A second emphasis of the SFS program is expansion of the U.S. higher education enterprise to produce cybersecurity professionals through a variety of efforts. These include research on the teaching and learning of cybersecurity, development of curricula, integrating cybersecurity topics into relevant degree programs, developing virtual laboratories, strengthening partnerships between government and relevant employment sectors to better integrate applied research experiences into cybersecurity degree programs, and integrating data science into cybersecurity curricula.

From FY 2011 through FY 2014, the SFS program made 117 awards throughout the U.S., totaling over $145 million. As of early August 2015, the SFS program has provided scholarships to more than 2,400 students and graduated more than 1,700, including 22 percent with bachelor's degrees, 76 percent with master's degrees, and two percent with doctoral degrees. Of these graduates, 93 percent have been successfully placed in the Federal Government. SFS scholarship recipients have been placed in internships and full-time positions in more than 140 Federal departments, agencies, and branches, including the NSA, DHS, Central Intelligence Agency, and Department of Justice, along with state, local, and tribal governments.

The SFS program has recently embarked on a new activity, Inspiring the Next Generation of Cyber Stars (or GenCyber) summer camps, to seed the interest of young people in this exciting and exploding new field, to help them learn about cybersecurity, and to learn how skills in this area could pay off for them in the future. These overnight and day camps are available to students and teachers at the K–12 level at no expense to them; funding is provided by NSF and NSA. A pilot project for cybersecurity summer camps in 2014 stimulated such great interest that the GenCyber program expanded in 2015, supporting 43 camps held on 29 university campuses in 19 states with more than 1,400 participants.

I would like to highlight the fact that Dakota State University (DSU) has successfully competed for an NSF award to develop greater capacity for cybersecurity education, and for two scholarship grants to support cybersecurity students. Of the students who were awarded scholarships in the cybersecurity program at DSU, about half have graduated and all have been placed in government cybersecurity jobs; half are still in school; and a new cohort of scholarship holders is anticipated in the fall of 2015. In addition, DSU ran two GenCyber camps in 2015, one for high school students entering grades 10–12, and one for girls entering grades 8–12. You have heard additional detail about NSF-funded cybersecurity activities at DSU from other witnesses here today.

Strategic Planning Across the Federal Government

Finally, NSF closely coordinates its activities with other Federal agencies and collaborates with them in pursuing cybersecurity research and education activities. In 2011, the National Science and Technology Council (NSTC), with the cooperation of NSF, developed a strategic plan titled *Trustworthy Cyberspace: Strategic Plan for the Federal Cybersecurity Research and Development Program.*[4] This plan has guided coordination across the Federal Government. As you know, the 2014 Cybersecurity Enhancement Act called for an updated R&D strategic plan. NSF is playing a key role in developing the revision of the strategic plan. Recognizing the changes in the threats to the national economy and security posed by cyber attacks, the revised strategy will expand on the 2011 report, with increased focus on areas including privacy, security of the Internet of Things and Cyber-Physical Systems, and an increased breadth of the understanding of human-centric aspects (social, behavioral, cultural, and psychological) of cybersecurity. Without deep awareness of the latter dimensions, a purely technological solution to cybersecurity is likely to fail.

Coordination Across the Federal Government

NSF coordinates its cybersecurity research and planning activities with other Federal agencies, including the Department of Defense (DoD) and DHS, and the agencies of the intelligence community, through various "mission-bridging" activities:

- NSF plays a leadership role in the interagency Networking and Information Technology Research and Development (NITRD) program. The National Science and Technology Council's NITRD Subcommittee, of which NSF is co-chair, has played a prominent role in coordinating the Federal Government's cybersecurity research investments.

- A NITRD Senior Steering Group (SSG) for Cyber Security and Information Assurance R&D (CSIA R&D)[5] was established to provide a responsive and robust conduit for cybersecurity R&D information across the policy, fiscal, and research levels of the government. The SSG is composed of senior representatives of agencies with national cybersecurity leadership positions, including: NSF, DoD, the Office of the Director of National Intelligence (ODNI), DHS, NSA, the National Institute of Standards and Technology (NIST), the Office of Science and Technology Policy, and the Office of Management and Budget. A principal responsibility of the SSG is to define, coordinate, and recommend strategic Federal R&D objectives in cybersecurity, and to communicate research needs and proposed budget priorities to policy makers and budget officials.

- To facilitate conversation among classified and unclassified programs in the Federal Government, a coordinating group called Special Cyber Operations Research and Engineering (SCORE) was established. SCORE includes members from the CSIA R&D Senior Steering Group. NSF research, which is non-classified, is reported in this forum.

- On the education front, NSF is an active participant and contributor in the NIST-led National Initiative for Cybersecurity Education (NICE). NSF's involvement aims to bolster formal cybersecurity education programs encompassing K–12, higher education, and vocational programs, with a focus on the science, technology, engineering, and math disciplines to provide a pipeline of skilled workers for the private sector and government.

Conclusions

Our Nation must continue to invest in long-term, fundamental, and game-changing research if our cyber systems are to remain trustworthy in the future. NSF's interdisciplinary research and education portfolios are contributing to a next-generation workforce that is increasingly cyber-aware, armed with the knowledge that it needs to protect against cyber attacks. With robust, sustained support for cybersecurity research and education in both the executive and legislative branches, as well as partnerships such as those on display here at Dakota State University, NSF contributes to the protection of our national security and the enhancement of our economic prosperity. This concludes my remarks. I would be happy to answer any questions at this time.

———

BIOGRAPHICAL SKETCH

Mr. Jeremy Epstein is the Lead Program Director for the National Science Foundation's (NSF) Secure and Trustworthy Cyberspace (SaTC) program, the Federal Government's flagship fundamental cybersecurity research program. In addition to

[4] *http://www.whitehouse.gov/sites/default/files/microsites/ostp/fed_cybersecurity_rd_strategic_plan_2011.pdf*
[5] *https://www.nitrd.gov/nitrdgroups/index.php?title=Cyber_Security_Information_Assurance_Research_and_Development_Senior_Steering_Group_%28CSIA_R%26D_SSG%29*

SaTC, he leads the Computer and Information Science and Engineering (CISE) Research Initiation Initiative (CRII) and co-leads the NSF/Intel Partnership on Cyber-Physical Systems Security and Privacy (CPS-Security) within NSF's CISE Directorate. Jeremy's research areas include software security and voting systems security. He is associate editor-in-chief of the IEEE Security & Privacy Magazine; founder of the Applied Computer Security Associates (ACSA) Scholarships for Women Studying Information Security (SWSIS); the IEEE representative to the NIST Technical Guidelines Development Committee which writes voting systems standards; and a senior member of IEEE and ACM. He holds an M.S. in computer sciences from Purdue University and a B.S. from the New Mexico Institute of Mining and Technology.

The CHAIRMAN. Thank you, Mr. Epstein.

We will move on now to—I am sorry, got you guys on opposite sides here—to Mr. Stine.

Please proceed.

STATEMENT OF KEVIN STINE, LEADER, SECURITY OUTREACH AND INTEGRATION GROUP, COMPUTER SECURITY DIVISION, INFORMATION TECHNOLOGY LABORATORY, NATIONAL INSTITUTE OF STANDARDS AND TECHNOLOGY, U.S. DEPARTMENT OF COMMERCE

Mr. STINE. Thank you, Chairman Thune and members of Dakota State University.

I will shorten the business card a little bit and just say that I am Kevin Stine, leader of the Security Outreach and Integration Group at the National Institute of Standards and Technology, which is better known as NIST. I will add to the business card that we are part of the U.S. Department of Commerce, which puts us at an interesting intersection point between government and industry and academia, as well, especially in the cybersecurity space.

Thank you for the opportunity to discuss NIST's role in confronting the challenge of cybersecurity.

NIST's role in cybersecurity was authorized in 1972 with the Brooks Act and continues today through FISMA, as well as the recent authorities under the Cybersecurity Enhancement Act of 2014, to develop key cybersecurity guidelines for protecting U.S. Government information and information systems.

On behalf of NIST, I wanted to thank the Chairman for his steadfast leadership on this issue.

It is important to note that the impact of NIST's activities extends beyond providing the means to protect Federal information and information systems. Many organizations outside the Federal Government voluntarily follow NIST standards and guidelines, reflecting their wide acceptance throughout the world.

NIST accomplishes its mission in cybersecurity through collaborative partnerships with our customers and stakeholders in industry, government, academia, standards bodies, consortia, and international organizations. These collaborative efforts are constantly being expanded by new initiatives, including in recent years through four major programs which I will briefly describe.

The first program is the National Strategy for Trusted Identities in Cyberspace, or NSTIC, where NIST works to address security issues surrounding the inadequacy of passwords. In a 2013 industry report, it was reported that 76 percent of network intrusions exploited weak or stolen credentials. Many recent examples of breaches, which you have heard about in the news, fall in line with the findings of that report.

The second program is the National Cybersecurity Center of Excellence, of the NCCoE, which is a partnership between NIST, the state of Maryland, Montgomery County, Maryland, and the private sector to accelerate the adoption of solutions to cybersecurity challenges by working directly with businesses across various industry sectors on solutions to those cybersecurity challenges.

Current activities are addressing challenges in the healthcare, retail, financial services, and energy sectors, as well as looking at security issues around cloud security, identity management, mobile devices, and secure e-mail.

The third NIST program is the National Initiative for Cybersecurity Education, or NICE, which works to meet the needs of the U.S. workforce by promoting an ecosystem of cybersecurity education, training, and workforce development to secure cyberspace by accelerating learning and skills development, nurturing a diverse learning environment, and guiding career development and workforce planning.

The fourth program is the Framework for Improving Critical Infrastructure Cybersecurity, called for in Executive Order 13–636. The framework, issued over one year ago, was created through collaboration with industry, government, and academia and consists of standards, guidelines, and practices to help organizations understand, communicate, and manage cybersecurity risks to critical infrastructure.

NIST is also tasked with the key role of coordinating Federal agency use of voluntary consensus standards and participation in the development of relevant standards, as well as promoting coordination between the public and private sectors in the development of standards and in conformity assessment activities.

The U.S. standards system differs significantly from the government-led systems common in many other countries. Under the U.S. system, hundreds of standards-developing organizations provide the infrastructure for standards, with NIST playing a key role as facilitator and technical advisor in the process.

NIST also conducts cybersecurity research and development in forward-looking technology areas, such as the security for smartcards, the information and communications technology supply chain, mobile devices and applications, cyber physical systems, and public safety networks, and the usability of systems, including electronic health records and voting machines.

We at NIST recognize that we have an essential role to play in helping industry, consumers, and government to counter cyber threats. We are extremely proud of our role in establishing and improving the comprehensive set of cybersecurity technical solutions, standards, guidelines, and best practices and the robust collaborations with our Federal Government partners, private-sector and academic collaborators, and international colleagues.

Again, I thank you for the opportunity to testify today on NIST's work in cybersecurity, and I would be happy to answer any questions you may have.

[The prepared statement of Mr. Stine follows:]

PREPARED STATEMENT OF KEVIN STINE, LEADER, SECURITY OUTREACH AND INTEGRATION GROUP, COMPUTER SECURITY DIVISION, INFORMATION TECHNOLOGY LABORATORY, NATIONAL INSTITUTE OF STANDARDS AND TECHNOLOGY, U.S. DEPARTMENT OF COMMERCE

Introduction

Chairman Thune, members of the Committee, I am Kevin Stine, Leader of the Security Outreach and Integration Group in the Computer Security Division, Information Technology Laboratory (ITL) at the Department of Commerce's National Institute of Standards and Technology (NIST). Thank you for the opportunity to appear before you today to discuss NIST's role in confronting the challenge of cybersecurity.

The Role of NIST in Cybersecurity

With programs focused on national priorities from the Smart Grid and electronic health records to forensics, atomic clocks, advanced nanomaterials, computer chips and more, NIST's overall mission is to promote U.S. innovation and industrial competitiveness by advancing measurement science, standards, and technology in ways that enhance economic security and improve our quality of life.

In the area of cybersecurity, NIST has worked with Federal agencies, industry, and academia since 1972, starting with the development of the Data Encryption Standard, when the potential commercial benefit of this technology became clear. NIST's role, to research, develop and deploy information security standards and technology to protect the Federal Government's information systems against threats to the confidentiality, integrity and availability of information and services, was strengthened through the Computer Security Act of 1987 (Public Law 100–235), broadened through the Federal Information Security Management Act of 2002 (FISMA; 44 U.S.C. § 3541 et seq.) and recently reaffirmed in the Federal Information Security Modernization Act of 2014 (Public Law 113–283). In addition, the Cybersecurity Enhancement Act of 2014 (Public Law 113–274) authorizes NIST to facilitate and support the development of voluntary, industry-led cybersecurity standards and best practices for critical infrastructure. On behalf of NIST, I want to thank the Chairman for his steadfast leadership on this issue. The bill could not have been enacted into law without his efforts.

NIST accomplishes its mission in cybersecurity through collaborative partnerships with our customers and stakeholders in industry, government, academia, standards bodies, consortia and international partners. NIST employs these collaborative partnerships to take advantage of the technical and operational insights of our partners and to leverage the resources of a global community. These collaborative efforts, and our private sector collaborations in particular, are constantly being expanded by new initiatives, including in recent years through the National Strategy for Trusted Identities in Cyberspace (NSTIC), the National Cybersecurity Center of Excellence (NCCoE), the National Initiative for Cybersecurity Education (NICE), and through the implementation of the Obama Administration's Executive Order 13636, "Improving Critical Infrastructure Cybersecurity." These programs and others are supported by and implemented through NIST's cybersecurity research, standards, and guidelines.

NIST Cybersecurity Research, Standards, and Guidelines

NIST Special Publications and Interagency Reports provide management, operational, and technical security guidelines for Federal agency information systems, and cover a broad range of topics such as Basic Input/Output System (BIOS) management and measurement, key management and derivation, media sanitization, electronic authentication, security automation, Bluetooth and wireless protocols, incident handling and intrusion detection, malware, cloud computing, public key infrastructure, risk assessments, supply chain risk management, online identity, authentication, access control, privacy risk management, security automation and continuous monitoring.

Beyond these documents—which are peer-reviewed throughout industry, government, and academia—NIST conducts workshops, awareness briefings, and outreach to ensure comprehension of standards and guidelines, to share ongoing and future activities, and to aid in scoping guidelines in a collaborative, open, and transparent manner.

In addition, NIST maintains the National Vulnerability Database (NVD), a repository of standards-based vulnerability management reference data. The NVD makes available information on vulnerabilities, impact measurements, detection techniques, and remediation assistance. It provides reference data that enable government, industry and international security automation capabilities. The NVD also assists/helps/enables the Payment Card Industry (PCI) to identify and mitigate

13

vulnerabilities. The PCI uses the NVD vulnerability metrics to discern the IT vulnerability in point-of-sale devices and determine what risks are unacceptable for that industry.

Pursuant to the Cybersecurity Research and Development Act of 2002, NIST also maintains a library of security setting configurations, also known as "checklists," for IT products used throughout the Federal Government. This initiative is known as the National Checklist Program. Through the program, product vendors, as well as Federal contributors, supply checklists to be quality assured by NIST and peer-reviewed by the public, with the final benchmarks cataloged by NIST and made available as reference data for both government and the private sector. One of the more prominent examples of a checklist is the United States Government Configuration Baseline, or USGCB. To produce a USGCB, Federal checklist contributors work with the Federal CIO Council and NIST to determine government-wide security settings. The resulting USGCB checklists are made available to all parties through the National Checklist Program.

NIST researchers develop and standardize cryptographic mechanisms that are used throughout the world to protect information at rest and in transit. These mechanisms provide security services, such as confidentiality, integrity, authentication, non-repudiation and digital signatures, to protect sensitive information. The NIST algorithms and associated cryptographic guidelines are developed in a transparent and inclusive process, leveraging cryptographic expertise around the world. The results are in standard, interoperable cryptographic mechanisms that can be used by all industries. For example, with approval of the Secretary of Commerce, NIST recently published Federal Information Processing Standard (FIPS) 202, which specifies the SHA–3 family of hash functions that provide many important information security applications, including the generation and derivation of digital signatures.

NIST has a complementary program, in coordination with the Government of Canada, to certify independent commercial calibration laboratories to test commercially available IT cryptographic modules, to ensure that they have implemented the NIST cryptographic standards and guidelines correctly. These testing laboratories exist around the globe and test hundreds of individual cryptographic modules yearly.

Recently, NIST initiated a research program in usability of cybersecurity, focused on passwords and password policies; user perceptions of cybersecurity risk and privacy concerns; and privacy in general. The concept of "usability" refers generally to "the effectiveness, efficiency, and satisfaction with which the intended users can achieve their tasks in the intended context of product use." [1] This usability research will lead to standards and guidelines for improving cybersecurity through increased attention to user interactions with security technologies.

NIST Engagement with Government

In support of FISMA implementation, NIST continues its collaboration with the Department of Defense, the intelligence community, and the Committee on National Security Systems, through a Joint Task Force Initiative, to develop key cybersecurity guidelines for protecting U.S. Government information and information systems.

This collaboration allows the most broad-based and comprehensive set of safeguards and countermeasures ever developed for information systems. This unified framework of guidelines and recommendations provides a standardized method for expressing security at all levels, from operational implementation to compliance reporting. It allows for an environment of information sharing and interconnections among these communities and significantly reduces costs, time, and resources needed for finite sets of systems and administrators to report on cybersecurity to multiple authorities.

Our set of standards, guidelines, and recommendations provide a standardized and repeatable framework for managing risk, called the Risk Management Framework. The Risk Management Framework provides a structured, yet flexible, approach for managing the risk resulting from using information systems to achieve the mission and business processes of an organization. The risk management concepts are intentionally broad-based with the specific details of assessing risk and employing appropriate risk mitigation strategies provided by supporting NIST information security standards and guidelines.

This approach allows for implementation of cost-effective, risk-based information security programs. It establishes a level of security due diligence for Federal agencies and contractors supporting the Federal Government. It creates a consistent and cost-effective application of security controls across an information technology infra-

---

[1] ISO 9241–210:2010, *Ergonomics of human-system interaction—Part 210: Human-centered design for interactive systems.*

structure and a consistent, comparable, and repeatable security control assessment. When implemented, it gives an organization a better understanding of enterprise-wide mission risks resulting from the operation of information systems.

NIST Engagement with Industry

It is important to note that the impact of NIST's activities under FISMA extend beyond providing the means to protect Federal IT systems. They provide the cybersecurity foundations for the public trust that is essential to our realization of the national and global productivity and innovation potential of electronic business and its attendant economic benefits. Many organizations voluntarily follow NIST standards and guidelines, reflecting their wide acceptance throughout the world.

Beyond NIST's responsibilities under FISMA, under the provisions of the National Technology Transfer and Advancement Act (PL 104–113) and related OMB Circular A–119, NIST is tasked with the key role of coordinating Federal agency use of voluntary consensus standards and participation in the development of relevant standards, as well as promoting coordination between the public and private sectors in the development of standards and in conformity assessment activities. NIST works with other agencies, such as the Departments of Defense, State, and Homeland Security to coordinate positions on standards issues and priorities with the private sector through consensus standards organizations such as the American National Standards Institute (ANSI), the Joint Technical Committee 1 (JTC 1) of the International Organization for Standardization (ISO) and the International Electrotechnical Commission (IEC), the Institute of Electrical and Electronics Engineers (IEEE), the Internet Engineering Task Force (IETF), and the International Telecommunications Union's Standardization Sector (ITU–T).

NIST's partnership with industry to develop, maintain, and implement voluntary consensus standards related to cybersecurity best ensures the interoperability, security, and resiliency of the global infrastructure needed to make us all more secure. It also allows this infrastructure to evolve in a way that embraces both security and innovation—allowing a market to flourish to create new types of secure products for the benefit of all Americans.

NIST works extensively in smart card standards, guidelines, and best practices. NIST developed the standard for the U.S. Government Personal Identity Verification (PIV) Card (FIPS 201), and actively works with the ANSI and JTC 1 on global cybersecurity standards for use in smart cards, smart card cryptography and the standards for the international integrated circuit card. [ANSI 504; ISO 7816 and ISO 24727]

NIST also conducts cybersecurity research and development in forward looking technology areas, such as security for Federal mobile environments and techniques for measuring and managing information security. These efforts focus on improving the trustworthiness of IT components such as claimed identities, data, hardware, and software for networks and devices. Additional research areas include developing approaches to balancing safety, security, and reliability in the Nation's information and communications technology supply chain; enabling mobile device and application security; securing the Nation's cyber-physical systems and public safety networks; enabling continuous information security monitoring; providing advanced information security measurements and testing; investigating information security analytics and big data; developing standards, modeling, and measurements to achieve end-to-end information security over heterogeneous, multi-domain networks; and investigating technologies for detection of anomalous behavior and quarantines.

In addition, further development of cybersecurity standards will be needed to improve the security and resiliency of critical U.S. information and communication infrastructure. The availability of cybersecurity standards and associated conformity assessment schemes is essential in these efforts, which NIST supports, to help enhance the deployment of sound security solutions and build trust among those creating and those using the solutions throughout the country.

International Cybersecurity Standardization

The Cybersecurity Enhancement Act of 2014 directed NIST to work with relevant Federal agencies to ensure interagency coordination in "the development of international technical standards related to information system security" and "ensure consultation with appropriate private sector stakeholders." It also called for NIST to submit a plan for ensuring the Federal agency coordination to Congress within one year. The International Cybersecurity Standards Working Group, which is led by the Department of Commerce/NIST, was set up by the National Security Council's Cyber Interagency Policy Committee to draft this plan, which will also serve as the basis of the required report to Congress.

The U.S. standards system differs significantly from the government-directed and government-led systems common in many other countries. Under the U.S. system, hundreds of standards development organizations (SDOs) provide the infrastructure for the preparation of standards documents. While these organizations are overwhelmingly private sector, government personnel participate in standards development activities as equal partners along with representatives from industry, academia, and other organizations and consumers.

The new draft *Report on Strategic U.S. Government Engagement in International Standardization to Achieve U.S. Objectives for Cybersecurity* (NIST draft Interagency Report 8074)[2] and supplement lay out strategic objectives and recommendations for enhancing the U.S. government's coordination and participation in the development and use of international standards for cybersecurity. The draft report recommends the government make greater effort to coordinate the participation of its employees in international cybersecurity standards development to promote the cybersecurity and resilience of U.S. information and communications systems and supporting infrastructures.

A supplement[3] to the draft report provides a summary of ongoing activities in critical international cybersecurity standardization and an inventory of U.S. government and private sector engagement. It also provides guidance for agencies to plan and coordinate more effective participation in these activities.

The draft report supports the 2010 United States Standards Strategy,[4] which was developed through a public-private partnership and outlines the contribution of private-sector led standards development to overall competition and innovation in the U.S. economy and the imperative of public and private sector participation and collaboration.

National Strategy for Trusted Identities in Cyberspace

NIST also houses the National Program Office established to lead implementation of the National Strategy for Trusted Identities in Cyberspace (NSTIC). NSTIC is an initiative that works to address one of the most commonly exploited vectors of attack in cyberspace: the inadequacy of passwords for authentication.

Weak authentication and identity proofing methods continue to represent a disproportionate share of data breaches and other successful attacks. The 2013 Data Breach Investigations Report[5] noted that in 2012, 76 percent of network intrusions exploited weak or stolen credentials. In line with the results of this report, many recent high profile compromises involved weak or compromised credentials or weaknesses in identity proofing as the vector of attack.

NSTIC works to address this issue by collaborating with the private sector to catalyze a marketplace of better identity and authentication solutions—an "Identity Ecosystem" that raises the level of trust associated with the identities of individuals, organizations, networks, services, and devices online. NIST has funded 15 pilot programs to jumpstart the marketplace and test new approaches to overcome barriers, such as usability, privacy, and interoperability, which have hindered market acceptance and wider use of stronger authentication technologies.

NSTIC exemplifies NIST's robust collaboration with industry, in large part, because the initiative calls on the private sector to lead implementation. NIST has partnered with the privately led Identity Ecosystem Steering Group (IDESG) to craft better standards and tools to improve authentication online.

National Cybersecurity Center of Excellence

In 2012, NIST established the National Cybersecurity Center of Excellence (NCCoE). The NCCoE brings together experts from industry, government, and academia to develop and transfer practical cybersecurity standards, technologies, and best practices to the Nation's business sectors. By accelerating dissemination and use of standards, best practices, and integrated tools and technologies for protecting information technology assets and processes, the NCCoE fosters trust in U.S. business sectors and improvements to the overall security of the economy. The NCCoE supports implementation of existing cybersecurity guidelines and frameworks, serves as a technical resource for both public and private sectors, and contributes to the development of cybersecurity practices and practitioners.

---

[2] http://csrc.nist.gov/publications/drafts/nistir-8074/nistir_8074_vol1_draft_report.pdf
[3] http://csrc.nist.gov/publications/drafts/nistir-8074/nistir_8074_vol2_draft_supplemental-information.pdf
[4] http://publicaa.ansi.org/sites/apdl/Documents/Standards%20Activities/NSSC/USSS_Third_edition/USSS%202010-sm.pdf
[5] http://www.verizonenterprise.com/resources/reports/rp_data-breach-investigations-report-2013_en_xg.pdf

The NCCoE is a unique partnership among three levels of government: NIST at the Federal level, the State of Maryland, and Montgomery County, Maryland. In addition the NCCoE established a Federally Funded Research and Development Center (FFRDC), the country's first FFRDC dedicated to cybersecurity, which helps the center respond to national priorities and critical security concerns impacting critical infrastructure, e-commerce, and privacy.

To date, NIST has established partnerships with 22 industry partners who have pledged to have a continuous presence at the center as National Cybersecurity Excellence Partner (NCEP) companies. In addition to these core partners, there are more than 25 other technology companies that are working on projects at the NCCoE under Cooperative Research and Development Agreements (CRADAs). These partners and collaborators support the NCCoE with hardware, software, and expertise. They provide the Center equipment to outfit labs as real-world environments, and their personnel work at the NCCoE as guest researchers.

Today, the NCCoE has programs working with the health care, energy, financial services, and retail sectors. In addition, the Center is addressing challenges that cut across sectors, including mobile device security, software asset management, cloud security, identity management, and secure e-mail. The NCCoE's first practice guide,[6] released this summer for public comment, helps secure electronic health records on mobile devices. As both electronic medical records and mobile devices are increasingly used by health care practitioners, patient information needs to be protected to preserve privacy and safeguard identity and patient care. The NCCoE's practice guide, *Securing Electronic Health Records on Mobile Devices,* provides a detailed architecture and instructions so that IT professionals can recreate the security capabilities of the example solution. The guide does not recommend specific products, but provides a blueprint for the deployment and use of standards based technologies that address critical security concerns. The solution aligns to standards and best practices from NIST and to the Health Insurance Portability and Accountability Act Security Rule.

National Initiative for Cybersecurity Education

As the cybersecurity threat and technology environment evolves, the cybersecurity workforce must continue to adapt to design, develop, implement, maintain and continuously improve cybersecurity, including in our Nation's critical infrastructure.

Established in 2010, the National Initiative for Cybersecurity Education (NICE) promotes an ecosystem of cybersecurity education, training, and workforce development that effectively secures cyberspace. Led by NIST, NICE is a partnership between government, academia, and industry that builds upon existing successful programs, including the DHS/NSA Centers of Academic Excellence for Cybersecurity, and facilitates innovation to increase the supply of qualified cybersecurity workers.

NICE's emerging strategic priorities include accelerating learning and skills development, nurturing a diverse learning community, and guiding career development and workforce planning. NICE works to instill a sense of urgency in both the public and private sectors to address the skilled workforce shortage. It is also working to strengthen formal education programs, promote different academic pathways, and increase the participation of women, minorities, and veterans in the cybersecurity profession. Finally, it supports job seekers and employers to address market demands and maximize talent management.

NICE is also aligned with the President's Job-Driven Training Initiative and the Secretary of Commerce's Skills for Business Initiative that is partnering with business to equip workers for 21st century careers.

Cybersecurity Framework

Over one year ago, NIST issued the Framework for Improving Critical Infrastructure Cybersecurity (Framework)[7] in accordance with Section 7 of Executive Order 13636, "Improving Critical Infrastructure Cybersecurity."[8] The Framework, created through collaboration with industry, government, and academia, consists of standards, guidelines, and practices to promote the protection of critical infrastructure. The prioritized, flexible, repeatable, and cost-effective approach of the Framework helps owners and operators of critical infrastructure to manage cybersecurity-related risk. Since the release of the Framework, NIST has strengthened its collaborations with critical infrastructure owners and operators, industry leaders, government partners, and other stakeholders to raise awareness about the Framework, en-

---

[6] *https://nccoe.nist.gov/projects/use_cases/health_it/ehr_on_mobile_devices*
[7] *http://www.nist.gov/cyberframework/upload/cybersecurity-framework-021214.pdf*
[8] *https://www.whitehouse.gov/the-press-office/2013/02/12/executive-order-improving-critical-infrastructure-cybersecurity*

courage use by organizations across and supporting the critical infrastructure, and develop implementation guides and resources. The Framework continues to be voluntarily implemented by industry and adopted by infrastructure sectors, which is contributing to reducing cyber risks to our Nation's critical infrastructure.

NIST supports Framework awareness and understanding by addressing a variety of sectors and communities through speaking engagements and meetings. NIST continues to educate other nations about the value of the Framework and the processes by which it was developed. Many of those nations are adopting Framework principles into equivalent national frameworks, while some are adopting the Framework in its entirety. To better support industry understanding and use, NIST is now publishing frequently asked questions and industry resources at the Framework Website.[9]

Pursuant to the Cybersecurity Enhancement Act of 2014, NIST also convened meetings with regulators to discuss application of the Framework within the cyber ecosystem, and the need for the Framework to remain a voluntary methodology, adaptable to the critical infrastructure risk and mission objectives. NIST participated in an advisory role to the Federal Communications Commission (FCC) Communications, Security, Reliability and Interoperability Council's (CSRIC) Working Group 4. NIST is also an advisory member of the Cybersecurity Forum for Independent and Executive Branch Regulators. The forum was chartered to increase the overall effectiveness and consistency of regulatory authorities' cybersecurity efforts pertaining to U.S. Critical Infrastructure. In all of these interactions, NIST continues to communicate the merits of the voluntary Framework as an organizational and communication tool to better manage cybersecurity risk.

Additional Research Areas

NIST performs research and development in related technologies, such as the usability of systems including electronic health records, voting machines, biometrics and software interfaces. NIST is performing research on the mathematical foundations needed to determine the security of information systems. In the areas of digital forensics, NIST is enabling improvements in forensic analysis through the National Software Reference Library and computer forensics tool testing. Software assurance metrics, tools, and evaluations developed at NIST are being implemented by industry to help strengthen software against hackers. NIST responds to government and market requirements for biometric standards by collaborating with other Federal agencies, academia, and industry partners to develop and implement biometrics evaluations, enable usability, and develop standards (fingerprint, face, iris, voice/speaker, and multimodal biometrics). NIST plays a central role in defining and advancing standards, and collaborating with customers and stakeholders to identify and reach consensus on cloud computing standards.

Conclusion

We at NIST recognize that we have an essential role to play in helping industry, consumers and government to counter cyber threats. Our broader work in the areas of information security, trusted networks, and software quality is applicable to a wide variety of users, from small and medium enterprises to large private and public organizations, including Federal Government agencies and companies involved with critical infrastructure.

We are extremely proud of our role in establishing and improving the comprehensive set of cybersecurity technical solutions, standards, guidelines, and best practices and the robust collaborations with our Federal Government partners, private sector collaborators, and international colleagues.

Thank you for the opportunity to testify today on NIST's work in cybersecurity. I would be happy to answer any questions you may have.

————

KEVIN STINE

Mr. Kevin Stine is the Leader of the Security Outreach and Integration Group in the Information Technology Laboratory's Computer Security Division at the National Institute of Standards and Technology. In this capacity, he oversees NIST collaborations with industry, academia, and government on the mission-specific application of security standards, guidelines, and technologies to help organizations understand and manage cybersecurity risk. This group develops technical cybersecurity guidelines and tools in diverse areas such as public safety communications; health information technology; smart grid, cyber physical, and industrial con-

---

[9] http://www.nist.gov/cyberframework/index.cfm

trol systems; supply chain risk management; and Federal agency cybersecurity programs. The group is also home to the National Initiative for Cybersecurity Education (NICE) and programs focused on cybersecurity outreach to small businesses, security education and training professionals, and Federal agencies. Recently, he led NIST's efforts to develop the Framework for Reducing Cybersecurity Risk to Critical Infrastructure (Cybersecurity Framework) as directed in Executive Order 13636. He is past chair of the Federal Computer Security Managers' Forum, which promotes sharing of information security practices among Federal agencies. He holds undergraduate degrees in Information Systems Management and Psychology from the University of Maryland, Baltimore County.

The CHAIRMAN. Thank you, Mr. Stine.
And we will flip it now to Mr. Shlanta.
Mark, welcome.

STATEMENT OF MARK SHLANTA, CHIEF EXECUTIVE OFFICER, SDN COMMUNICATIONS

Mr. SHLANTA. Chairman Thune, thank you. Thank you for inviting SDN to participate in today's field hearing.

SDN applauds your support of the voluntary framework developed by the National Institute of Standards and Technology, or NIST. The NIST Framework provides useful guidance to assist service providers, like SDN, in protecting their networks.

In addition, your Cybersecurity Enhancement Act took important steps to strengthen our Nation's cyber research, workforce development, and public awareness.

Dakota State University, an institution that has distinguished itself as a leader in cybersecurity education, is the perfect venue to host this discussion.

As we sit here in South Dakota, cybersecurity is not a problem limited by geography or to high-profile retailers, financial institutions, and the Federal Government. Anyone using technology is a target. It can be daunting for individuals, businesses, and at all levels of government to navigate how they can best reduce their risk.

Last year, SDN investigated 4,500 threats against its customers. Each threat ranged from one to several thousand separate attacks.

Let me share one example of an SDN customer. They are a small business that manufactures wire twist ties for packaging. And who would think of a company like that as a target of a cyber attack? Yet, last year, attackers used more than 100 different attack methods to try breaking into that company's network. SDN observed the malicious traffic coming from as far away as Brazil. Fortunately, our cybersecurity team halted these attacks with our Managed Firewall service.

In addition to that product, SDN offers a host of services that defend against cyber threats. We provide secure data storage, remote network monitoring, and managed router services.

SDN is in the process of deploying a new product to protect against Distributed Denial of Service attacks, or DDOS. A DDOS attack, sometimes also known as "D-D-O-S," is a type of attack that disables an online service by flooding it with massive amounts of data traffic.

Sometimes DDOS attackers warn their targets or are even boastful. I have an example here. Here is a screenshot of a Twitter post from this past July that warns of a pending attack.

19

The next slide shows the attacker announcing a "target list." The next day, the attacker released a long list of Federal, state, and local government targets. The domain names of our state government and the City of Sioux Falls were included on this list. This is a real-life example showing that we in South Dakota are not immune to cyber attacks.

Providers like SDN offer cybersecurity products that can reduce risk. The story, however, does not end there. Businesses have a responsibility to enforce internal security controls. Human error accounts for 95 percent of all security incidents. Businesses should therefore improve the cyber literacy of their work force, limit access to sensitive information, and take necessary steps to properly maintain their equipment, software, and websites.

SDN has reviewed and continues to study the NIST Framework and the sector-specific guidance from the FCC's Communications Security, Reliability, and Interoperability Council, or CSRIC. The CSRIC guidance provides a useful tool to help communications providers utilize the NIST Framework. Although the Framework has been available since last year, the CSRIC guidance was only released in March. It will take time for small and regional rural operators to fully digest and put these recommendations into practice.

While I applaud these efforts, it is important to remember that SDN, like many small and regional providers, already works hard to maintain a secure network. That being said, only one thing is certain when it comes to cybersecurity, and that is the job is never done. As such, we are continuing to review the Framework and the CSRIC guidance and will utilize both tools to strengthen our existing cybersecurity programs.

I encourage you to maintain your support for a voluntary, flexible, scalable approach to cybersecurity risk management. This approach is more effective than hard-line regulation that would struggle to keep pace with new and evolving threats. The Federal Government should encourage utilization of the NIST framework through outreach and education.

It is important to note that some small operators may need additional assistance, such as one-on-one technical support, to help them apply the Framework to their unique operations.

In closing, I thank you again for inviting SDN to participate in today's hearing. Cybersecurity is a responsibility that each of us has an obligation to uphold.

Thank you, Chairman Thune, for your leadership in the U.S. Senate and for convening today's hearing.

With that, I will welcome your questions.

[The prepared statement of Mr. Shlanta follows:]

PREPARED STATEMENT OF MARK SHLANTA, CHIEF EXECUTIVE OFFICER, SDN COMMUNICATIONS

Thank you, Senator Thune, for inviting SDN[1] to participate in today's field hearing. It is an honor to join this esteemed panel of experts to discuss the actions that should be taken to address the cyber threats facing our state and nation.

---

[1] SDN Communications ("SDN") is the premier business-to-business broadband service provider in South Dakota and southern Minnesota with a fiber optic network connecting eight states with high-speed broadband Internet and Wide Area Network (WAN) connectivity. In

Continued

We applaud Senator Thune for his support of the voluntary framework that was developed by industry stakeholders and the National Institute of Standards and Technology (NIST). Our national and economic security depends upon the reliable functioning of critical infrastructure.[2] The communications industry represents one of the 16 critical infrastructure sectors.[3] The NIST Framework provides useful guidance and best practices to assist critical infrastructure operators in protecting their networks. In addition to codifying this successful process, Senator Thune's "Cybersecurity Enhancement Act" took important steps to increase our Nation's commitment to cyber research, workforce development, and raising public awareness.[4]

The title of today's hearing, "Confronting the Challenge of Cybersecurity," gets to the heart of this pervasive and constantly evolving threat. Cybersecurity is not a problem limited to high-profile retailers, financial institutions, or the Federal Government. It is widespread. Any individual or organization using technology is a target. It can be daunting for individuals, businesses, and all levels of government to navigate how they can best reduce their risk.

It was appropriate to host this discussion at Dakota State University (DSU), an academic institution that has distinguished itself as a national leader in cybersecurity education. The National Security Agency (NSA) and Department of Homeland Security designated DSU as one of the Nation's first National Centers of Academic Excellence.[5] This summer, DSU, with support from the NSA and National Science Foundation, hosted a camp to get more young women interested in cybersecurity careers. When the 60 available spots quickly filled, SDN sponsored 40 additional participants. Like other operators of critical infrastructure, SDN relies upon a strong pipeline of skilled workers, and we are lucky to have many DSU graduates on our team. Prioritizing continued workforce development in the field of cybersecurity is an important national objective.

It feels like it has become nearly impossible to turn on the news without learning of yet *another* company or Federal department that has been compromised. We hear about the high-profile attacks against companies like Sony, Target, Anthem, Home Depot, and JPMorgan Chase, and many small and regional businesses assume this is a problem targeting only large companies. Unfortunately, we here in South Dakota are not immune to this threat.

SDN sees a large number of threats against its own network and customers each day. SDN quarantines about half the e-mails directed toward its domain. Additionally, our company firewall blocks hundreds of unauthorized, malicious traffic attempts each day. We observed nearly 4,500 threats against SDN customers within a single year. Each of these threats ranged from one to several thousand separate attacks.

Bedford Industries is a small business, based in Worthington, MN, that subscribes to SDN's cybersecurity services. The company manufactures wire twist ties and other packaging equipment. Although an outside observer might question why Bedford would be a target, SDN's cybersecurity threat report tells a different story. In the past year, SDN successfully halted more than 100 types of cyberattacks against Bedford—ultimately mitigating over 5,300 separate incidents. In layman's terms, this means attackers tried to break into Bedford's network 5,300 times using 100 different attack methods. Some of the threats were launched by attackers in the United States, but others originated as far away as Brazil.

SDN offers a host of security services to counter cyber threats targeting businesses in South Dakota and the surrounding region. We provide secure data storage at our LaMesa Data Center that protects health care, financial, and other sensitive information. We also offer around-the-clock remote network monitoring that detects and responds to unusual, potentially malicious activity on customer equipment and networks. Our managed firewall service blocks harmful malware to prevent viruses

---

2014, SDN became an owner and the managing partner for Southern Minnesota Broadband, LLC, which extends SDN's fiber network across southern Minnesota. SDN also provides networking equipment, phone systems, and managed solutions, including security, routers, firewalls, remote network monitoring, and storage.

[2] "Framework for Improving Critical Infrastructure Cybersecurity," National Institute for Standards and Technology," page 1, February 12, 2014, *http://www.nist.gov/cyberframework/upload/cybersecurity-framework-021214-final.pdf.*

[3] "Critical Infrastructure Sectors," Department of Homeland Security, June 12, 2014, *http://www.dhs.gov/critical-infrastructure-sectors.*

[4] "Rockefeller, Thune Statement on Passage of Commerce Cybersecurity Bill," Senator Thune Official Website, December 12, 2014, *http://www.thune.senate.gov/public/index.cfm/2014/12/rockefeller-thune-statement-on-passage-of-commerce-cybersecurity-bill.*

[5] "Centers of Academic Excellence Institutions," National Security Agency, July 8, 2015, *https://www.nsa.gov/ia/academic_outreach/nat_cae/institutions.shtml#sd.*

from entering a customer's network, and SDN's managed router service closes security gaps by ensuring devices are properly configured. Currently, a limited number of business broadband customers subscribe to these managed services, and their networks subsequently face a heightened risk of cyberattack. Raising public awareness is key to strengthening our Nation's preparedness.

SDN is in the process of deploying a managed Distributed Denial of Service ("DDoS") protection product. DDoS is a type of attack that can disable an online service by overwhelming it with massive data traffic. A DDoS attacker controls numerous infected machines—often termed "zombies" or "botnets"—to generate the data volumes required to perpetrate an attack. In some instances, a DDoS attack is designed to disrupt the delivery of services and impede private and public business operations. On other occasions, it may be a diversionary tactic timed to coincide with a coordinated effort to break through network defenses.

There has been a dramatic rise in the number of DDoS threats occurring across the United States, including in South Dakota.[6] During SDN's early deployment of this product, we have detected malicious DDoS traffic targeting the networks of South Dakota businesses and state government. Just last week during a single 24-hour period, SDN's technical team detected 105 possible malicious traffic patterns.[7] A 25-gigabit attack is the largest DDoS threat we have seen since launching the product.[8] To put this in perspective, a 25-gigabit attack would completely saturate a high-bandwidth business customer subscribing to a 10-gigabit Internet connection. A threat of this magnitude would take down or severely cripple the networks of most business customers in South Dakota.

Businesses are not the only organizations facing cybersecurity threats. South Dakota state and local governments, as well as our post-secondary education institutions, are regularly targeted by hacktivists and hackers. These attacks may involve DDoS threats. As previously described, a DDoS attack may be politically motivated, or it may represent a diversionary tactic working in concert with other efforts to infiltrate a network. Sometimes there is simply no clue as to why these attacks occur. On occasion, attackers warn their targets and are even boastful of their efforts. *Figure 1* and *Figure 2* include screenshots of Twitter posts from July 2015 warning of a forthcoming attack. *Figure 3* contains a "target list" of federal, state, and local government entities that the attacker has identified as targets. The domain names of the South Dakota state government and the City of Sioux Falls were included on the target list. These illustrative examples are attached as an appendix to this testimony.

Providers like SDN offer cybersecurity products that can reduce a company's cybersecurity risk. The story, however, does not end there. Businesses have a responsibility to establish and enforce internal security controls.[9] Employee error can

---

[6] "Q1 2015 State of the Internet—Security Report," State of the Internet Akamai Report, 2015, *https://www.stateoftheinternet.com/security-cybersecurity-ddos-mitigation.html*
"Trustwave Global Security Report," Trustwave, 2015, *https://www2.trustwave.com/rs/815-RFM-693/images/2015__TrustwaveGlobalSecurityReport.pdf*
[7] "DDoS Cybersecurity Threat Report for August 24, 2015," SDN Communications.
[8] "DDoS Cybersecurity Threat Report for August 19, 2015," SDN Communications.
There has been a dramatic rise in the number of DDoS attacks, with the incidents of attacks doubling between Q1 2014 and Q1 2015. While hacktivists and other organized cyberattack groups, such as Anonymous or the earlier LulzSec, launch politically motivated attacks impacting large corporations or governments, individual hackers can now easily initiate a cyberattack by subscribing to a DDoS for hire service. According to Trustwave's 2015 Global Security Report, DDoS attacks can be purchased starting at $5.00 an hour, $40.00 for 24 hours, or $900 for one month of attacks. A recent Incapsula survey of IT professionals from companies with 250 to over 10,000 employees determined that even a small DDoS attack can have major financial impacts on the targeted organization. The DDoS attack profile is shifting; while the bandwidth required to execute an attack has decreased, there has been an alarming increase in attack frequency and duration. With low barriers to entry and large dollar amounts at stake, DDoS attacks are on the rise. DDoS cyberattack protection has become critical for organizations dependent upon the Internet for conducting business.
[9] SDN has cybersecurity internal controls and policies in place to mitigate the company's risk of cyberattack. Businesses—both large and small—should adopt similar practices. While SDN has in-house expertise to operate its internal cybersecurity program, other businesses may opt to outsource this responsibility. For purpose of example, this footnote includes a general, non-comprehensive description of some internal cybersecurity procedures followed by SDN.
SDN protects its network with an enterprise firewall that enforces rules and only accepts traffic from approved external IP addresses. The company conducts daily and sometimes hourly antivirus definition updates to improve the detection of malicious software and prevent harmful downloads. Regular patches to SDN's operating system, PCs, and other devises close security gaps that could be exploited by an attacker. Any patch deemed critical to protecting our equipment and servers is performed immediately. The company enforces access policies that require

Continued

create major vulnerabilities. According to IBM's "2014 Cyber Security Intelligence Index," 95 percent of all security incidents involve human error.[10] Businesses should therefore improve the cyber-literacy of their workforce and limit their employees' access and ability to distribute sensitive information. Businesses should also take the necessary steps to properly configure and maintain their equipment, software, and websites to prevent vulnerabilities that can be exploited.

SDN works to adhere to security standards and best practices to protect the integrity of our network. For decades, we have been researching and incorporating industry and regulatory cybersecurity standards. We completed a Statement on Standards for Attestation Engagement No. 16 (SSAE 16) SOC I compliance report and audit and are currently working through the SSAE 16 SOC II security module. SDN enforces its policies governing how the company operates its network and manages access to its facilities. The company also utilizes security guidance from the Payment Card Industry (PCI) Data Security Standards, Health Insurance Portability and Accountability Act (HIPPA), the Federal Trade Administration's Red Flags Rule, and Customer Proprietary Network Information (CPNI).

SDN has reviewed and continues to study the NIST Framework and the sector-specific guidance from the Federal Communications Commission's Communications Security, Reliability, and Interoperability Council (CSRIC).[11] The NIST Framework helps shift our national focus from a "check-the-box" mentality towards a risk-based approach tailored to addressing and mitigating unique organizational risk.[12] This is a preferred, more effective approach than strict and prescriptive regulation that would struggle to keep up with emerging and constantly evolving threats. The CSRIC guidance provides a useful tool to help communications providers evaluate and utilize the Framework, and it includes tailored recommendations for small operators. Although the Framework has been available since last year, the CSRIC guidance was only recently released this past March. It will take time for small and regional rural operators to fully digest and put these recommendations into practice.

While I applaud these efforts, it is important to remember that SDN—like many small and regional providers in the rural telecom industry—already endeavors to maintain a secure communications network. SDN's cybersecurity program seeks to protect its core network and meet the needs of its customers. That being said, only one thing is certain when it comes to cybersecurity: the job is never done. As such, my legal and technical teams continue with their review of the NIST Framework and the CSRIC "best practices" guidance, and SDN plans to utilize both of these tools to strengthen its existing cybersecurity program.

As the Senate Commerce Committee continues monitoring the utilization of the NIST Framework, I encourage you to maintain your support for a voluntary, flexible, and scalable approach to cybersecurity risk management. The Federal Government should encourage utilization of the Framework through outreach and education to assist critical infrastructure operators in understanding, digesting, and implementing these practices. It is important to note that some small operators may need additional assistance, such as one-on-one technical support, to help them apply the Framework to their unique operations.

---

passwords to be regularly changed and pin codes and badges in order to enter physical locations. Virtual and physical locations are limited to the employees that require access in order to perform their job responsibilities. Cameras and door access logs are equipped throughout the company premise, and fingerprint entry is required at SDN's most secure locations.

SDN requires employees working remotely to utilize an SSL Virtual Private Network (VPN) and perform two-factor authentication to access the company's network. This encryption service masks all traffic between SDN's network and the end user. The company's local administrator policy and account usage monitoring prevents unsanctioned software downloads onto company-issued equipment. Limiting an employee's ability to download malicious software helps reduce the risk of social engineering attacks. SDN also blocks foreign devices from accessing its network using a Network Access Control (NAC) appliance to prevent unauthorized devices from connecting to the network. Outside laptops and mobile devices cannot connect to the company's private wifi network and are segregated onto a guest wifi network.

This represents a limited sample of the security procedures SDN has adopted to protect its internal business network.

[10] "IBM Security Services 2014 Cyber Security Intelligence Index: Analysis of cyber attack and incident data from IBM's worldwide security operations," IBM, June 2014, *http://www.slideshare.net/ibmsecurity/2014-cyber-security-intelligence-index.*

[11] "Cybersecurity Risk Management and Best Practices Working Group 4: Final Report, Communications Security, Reliability, and Interoperability Council, Federal Communications Commission, March 2015, *https://transition.fcc.gov/pshs/advisory/csric4/CSRIC_WG4_Report_Final_March_18_2015.pdf.*

[12] "Cyber Solutions Handbook," Booz Allen Hamilton, page 4, 2014, *http://www.boozallen.com/content/dam/boozallen/documents/Cyber-Solutions-Handbook.pdf.*

In closing, I want to thank you again for inviting SDN to participate in today's field hearing. Cybersecurity is a responsibility that each of us has an obligation to uphold. As individuals, we should take steps to increase our cyber literacy. As businesses—both large and small, we have a responsibility to maintain strong safeguards to protect our network and the sensitive consumer information we have been entrusted. Finally, it is vital that our government and operators of critical infrastructure continue bolstering their defenses against growing and rapidly evolving cyber threats.

Thank you, Senator Thune, for your leadership in the United States Senate and for convening today's hearing to discuss this important topic. With that, I welcome your questions.

APPENDIX

Figure 1.

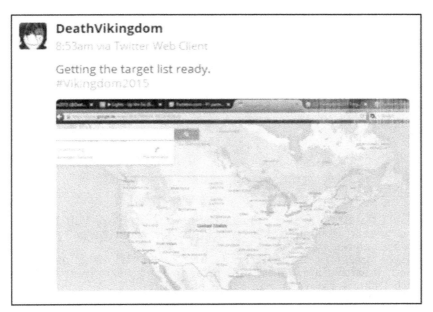

Figure 2.

Figure 3.

Texas.gov	brooklinems.gov	access-board.gov	uscourts.gov
louisiana.gov	cityofboston.gov	abilityone.gov	uscfc.uscourts.gov
arkansas.com	plymouth-ma.gov	acf.hhs.gov	akd.uscourts.gov
colorado.gov	ri.gov	acl.gov	azd.uscourts.gov
newmexico.gov	hartford.gov	ahrq.gov	catd.uscourts.gov
utah.gov	cityofmilford.com	bia.gov	ccd.uscourts.gov
oregon.gov	sumtercountyfl.gov	census.gov	ded.uscourts.gov
myflorida.com	sanfordfl.gov	publicdebt.treas.gov	flsd.uscourts.gov
michigan.gov	tompsc.com	idc.gov	gand.uscourts.gov
georgia.gov	cityofbr.org	treasury.gov	
alabama.gov	hartcountyga.gov	ed.gov	
iowa.gov	pentwater.org		
kentucky.gov	ci.minneapolis.mn.us		
illinois.gov	siouxfalls.org		
nebraska.gov	bit.indygov.org		
kansas.gov	naperville.il.us		
maryland.gov	cedar-rapids.org		
delaware.gov	desmoineswa.gov		
virginia.gov	columbus.gov		
maine.gov	columbus.in.gov		
visitnh.gov	bangormaine.gov		
ms.gov	sfgov.org		
nv.gov	seattle.gov		
sc.gov			
tn.gov			
ct.gov			
nj.gov			
pa.gov			
mo.gov			
in.gov			
wv.gov			
mn.gov			
nd.gov			
mt.gov			
sc.gov			
sd.gov			

The CHAIRMAN. Thank you, Mr. Shlanta. And we will look forward to talking about some of those issues when we get a chance to ask some questions.

And I am going to turn now to Mr. Eric Pulse, who, as I mentioned, is with Eide Bailly, but, prior to that, he is from Kimball, South Dakota. He was a Kimball Kiote, with a "K."

[Laughter.]

Mr. PULSE. Which doesn't exist anymore, by the way.

The CHAIRMAN. Which doesn't—yes, which doesn't exist anymore. I am a Jones County Coyote, with a "C."

[Laughter.]

The CHAIRMAN. But, anyway, he has a good, small-town heritage. And we welcome you to our committee this afternoon.

STATEMENT OF ERIC A. PULSE, PRINCIPAL, EIDE BAILLY, LLC

Mr. PULSE. Well, thank you, Chairman Thune. And thank you, DSU, for hosting this event. And thanks for the opportunity to appear here to discuss this topic of confronting the challenge of cybersecurity.

My testimony is based on my nearly 20 years in working with organizations and assessing and remediating and implementing their information systems and data security, cybersecurity controls.

NIST defines "cybersecurity" as the ability to protect or defend the use of cyberspace from cyber attacks. And the U.S. Department of Defense revealed that at the very top of the U.S. intelligence

25

community's 2013 assessment of global threats is cyber. That is ahead of terrorism and transnational organized crime.

The severity in impact of cyber threats have changed the landscape in which governments and corporations, individuals, and organizations of all industries, sizes, and complexities operate. The recent cyber-attack breaches on the U.S. Office of Personnel Management, Sony, Anthem, Home Depot, Target, J.P. Morgan—the list goes on, right?—simply emphasizes the importance of cybersecurity.

The Identity Theft Resource Center identified that, in 2015, through August 18, there have been a total of 505 reported data breaches, resulting in an estimated loss of nearly 100 million records. And that number is just the records known to be compromised.

Organizations spend millions of dollars on the latest security technologies and infrastructure to protect themselves from becoming the next organization in the news. However, cybersecurity is more than policies, procedures, and technologies; it has to be woven into the fabric of how each person, whether it is an employee or a customer, thinks about data security.

It begins with a culture. The best security standards, frameworks, policies, and procedures aren't able to anticipate every instance they are intended to facilitate. Security should be part of the fabric of every decision an employee makes in the course of everyday business.

Too often, organizations sacrifice sound security practices in the name of customer service or process efficiency. The extra step it may take to clearly verify a customer or gain that extra piece of information to validate the legitimacy of a person on the other end of a phone call, e-mail, or transaction is potentially overlooked because they were conditioned to provide exceptional customer service or were striving to be more efficient.

Simply put, security has taken a back seat, and that has to change. And that starts with an organizational culture. And, to be successful, the culture of IT has to be in sync with the organizational mission as a whole.

My written testimony highlights four areas that need attention in order to combat cybersecurity challenges: a security culture; the lack of skilled resources, which this great organization is working to fulfill; a framework, like the NIST framework; and threat intelligence.

After September 11, 2001, and the tragic events of that day, the way our society viewed air travel changed dramatically. It changed overnight. Restrictions on carry-on contents and long airport security lines are just a few restrictive and, to many degrees, necessary changes to air travel. On a flight in the months following that fateful day, a passenger near the rear of an aircraft proceeded to the front and nervously informed a flight attendant that he didn't feel safe because there was someone in a seat near him using a set of nail clippers. In short, our entire culture changed overnight, as it relates to air travel.

Conversely, in light of the many recent data breaches and identified hacks of government, civilian, private organizational systems, resulting in the loss of millions of data records, our society hasn't had the same necessary cultural shift. We tend to be nonchalant with sensitive data, whether it be credit cards for card-not-present transactions or participate in a drawing by filling out an entry form with personally identifiable information or disclosing health records or information as part of a survey.

Given the number of breaches that occur every day because someone clicked the proverbial phishing link in an e-mail scam, data is being compromised and identities are being stolen, millions of dollars are being lost. And yet we have yet to experience that cultural shift to better security practices.

In Verizon's 2015 Data Breach Investigations Report, it indicated that over 99 percent of all data breaches were successful exploits of vulnerabilities where the CVE, or the fix, the preventative fix, was over a year old. So nearly all breaches occur because a fix to an exploitable vulnerability was simply not applied.

This is particularly true with smaller organizations that continue to be targeted as attackers take advantage of frequently non-existent vulnerability and patch-management programs, exploiting weaknesses in edge devices, web-based apps, payment card or point-of-sale systems.

A recent survey by the SANS Institute showed that 66 percent of respondents cited a skills shortage as an impediment to effective incident response and overall cybersecurity. Many security professionals maintain a good general technical security skill set, tasked with implementing reasonable practices and procedures driven by compliance; however, the rise in advanced threats and malware demonstrate the need for a more sophisticated trained professional.

And, again, I want to thank you for allowing me to testify here today in our efforts to confront the challenges of cybersecurity. And, again, there are four areas that I think need increased attention, and those are: fostering a change in the security culture; an emphasis on increasing security personnel; encouraging an implementation of a common framework; and threat intelligence collaboration.

And thank you again for the opportunity.

[The prepared statement of Mr. Pulse follows:]

PREPARED STATEMENT OF ERIC A. PULSE, PRINCIPAL, EIDE BAILLY, LLP

Chairman Thune, Ranking Member Nelson, and distinguished members of the Committee. My name is Eric Pulse and I am a Principal with the accounting, tax and consulting firm Eide Bailly LLP and I am the director of our Risk Advisory Services practice, specializing in assisting clients with information, data, and cybersecurity needs. Thank you for the opportunity to appear before you today to discuss the topic of "Confronting the Challenge of Cybersecurity." My testimony today is based solely on my personal experiences over nearly 20 years working with clients assessing, remediating, and implementing their information systems, data and cybersecurity controls.

The National Institute of Standards and Technology (NIST) defines cybersecurity as "the ability to protect or defend the use of cyberspace from cyber-attacks." The U.S. Department of Defense revealed that "*at the top* of the U.S. intelligence community's 2013 assessment of global threats is cyber, followed by terrorism and transnational organized crime." The severity and impact of cyber threats have changed the landscape in which governments, corporations, individuals, and, organizations of all industries, size, and complexities operate. Breaches of customer data, credit card information, employee and customer authentication credentials, etc. are becoming more commonplace. This persistent threat is a societal issue facing everyone with personally identifiable information, health records, banking and/or payment information, intellectual property, etc. At one point considered largely an IT issue, the increase in frequency and sophistication of cyber attacks requires organizations elevate the priority to C-suites and board rooms and an overall cultural shift as it relates to cybersecurity.

The recent cyberattack breaches at U.S. Office of Personnel Management (OPM), Sony, Anthem, Home Depot, Target, JP Morgan, and many others simply emphasizes the importance of cybersecurity. The Identity Theft Resource Center[1] identified that in 2015, through August 18, there have been a total of 505 reported data breaches resulting in an estimated loss of nearly 140 million records—and that number is records *known* to be compromised. Organizations spend millions of dollars on the latest security technologies and infrastructure to protect themselves from becoming the next organization in the news. However, cybersecurity is more than policies, procedures and technologies. It has to be woven into the fabric of how each person, whether employee or customer, thinks about security of data. It begins with a culture. The best security standards, frameworks, policies or procedures aren't able to anticipate every instance they are intended to facilitate. Security should be a part of the fabric of every decision an employee makes in the course of everyday business. Too often organizations sacrifice sound security practices in the name of customer service or process efficiency. The extra step it may take to clearly verify a customer or gain that extra piece of information to validate the legitimacy of the person on the other end of the phone, e-mail, or transaction is overlooked because we are conditioned to provide exceptional customer service or we strive to be more efficient. Simply put, security has taken a back seat and that has to change. That change starts with organizational culture, and to be successful, a culture of IT security has to be in sync with the organizational mission as a whole.

I'd like to highlight four areas that need attention in order to combat cybersecurity challenges: a culture of security, the lack of skilled resources, a common framework, and threat intelligence.

Culture Shift

After September 11, 2001 and the tragic events of that day, the way our society viewed air travel changed dramatically. Restrictions on carry-on contents and long airport security lines are just a few restrictive, and to many degrees, necessary, changes to air travel. On a flight in the months following that fateful day, a passenger near the rear of an aircraft proceeded to the front and nervously informed the flight attendant that he didn't feel safe because there was someone in a seat near him using a set of nail clippers. In short, our entire culture changed overnight as it relates to air travel. Conversely, in light of the many recent data breaches and identified hacks of government, civilian, and private organizational computer systems, resulting in the loss of millions of data records, our society hasn't had the same necessary cultural shift. We are still nonchalant with our sensitive data, whether it be credit cards for card-not-present transactions, participating in a drawing by filling out an entry form with personally identifiable information, or by disclosing health records/information as part of a survey. Given the number of breaches that occur every day because someone clicked on the proverbial phishing link in an e-mail scam, data is being compromised, identities are being stolen, millions of dollars are being lost, and still we have yet to experience the cultural shock and shift to better security practices.

The first "hacker" to be charged and convicted of his crimes was Kevin Mitnick. He was able to effectively contact the companies to which he eventually gained access and simply ask for the access and it was granted. The crime was considered "fraudulent intent" and not the act of gaining access itself. This is still one of the leading threats to the security of organizations today and gets identified publically as an "insider threat." We lose site of the fact that most of the "insider" acts are unknown and unintentional, thus demonstrating the need for an enhanced security culture.

Verizon's 2015 Data Breach Investigations Report[2] indicates that over 99 percent of all data breaches were successful exploits of vulnerabilities where the CVE (Common Vulnerability and Exposure)—or preventative fix—was over one year old. Nearly all data breaches occur because a fix to an exploitable vulnerability was not applied. This is particularly true with smaller organizations that continue to be targeted as attackers take advantage of frequently non-existent vulnerability and patch management programs, exploiting weaknesses in edge devices, web-based applications, payment card or point of sale systems.

Smaller organizations face include the lack of technical feasibility to immediately apply a software patch that fixes a vulnerability because frequently, a security patch will negatively impact the functionality of a piece of software running on the device being patched. While vulnerability and patch management programs are an integral control in cybersecurity, the clients I serve span the spectrum, from mature,

28

highly integrated cybersecurity controls to non-existent controls where management has turned a blind eye in the interest of cost containment. The absence of a mature security culture and lack of cyber threat awareness emphasizes the need for further education at the highest organizational levels. The maturation of a security culture in the marketplace should start at the top in the boardrooms and continue with executive management driving it throughout their organizations.

Further educating the citizenry is also critical. Efforts like STOP.THINK. CONNECT by the National Cyber Security Alliance and the Department of Homeland Security highlight the importance of taking security precautions and understanding the consequences of actions and behaviors in order to enjoy the benefits of the Internet. I believe more visible efforts are necessary in order to educate a vast majority of people who simply take for granted the security of their personal and protected information.

Skills Gap

A recent survey by the SANS Institute[3] showed that 66 percent of respondents cited skills shortage as an impediment to effective incident response and overall cybersecurity. Many security professionals maintain a general technical security skillset tasked with implementing reasonable practices and procedures driven by compliance, however the rise in advanced threats and malware demonstrate the need for a more sophistically trained professional. This shortfall is reflected in my own daily experiences, whether it is with our clients or our firm, we are continually looking for personnel with the proper technical security skillset. The law of supply and demand has driven up the cost of these resources and many organizations simply cannot afford them, if they are even available. Many of the clients with which I work have opted to outsource many of these security functions given the limited availability of these skillsets. Heretofore, many security professionals contain a general technical security skillset tasked with implementing reasonable practices and procedures driven by compliance, however the rise in advanced threats and malware demonstrate the need for a more sophistically trained professional.

According to a poll conducted by Information Systems Audit and Control Association (ISACA) and the RSA Conference, and published in the "State of Cybersecurity: Implications for 2015" study, more than half of the global cybersecurity professionals polled reported that fewer than 25 percent of cybersecurity applicants are qualified to perform the skills needed for the job.[4]

I commend institutions like Dakota State University (DSU), and the initiation and evolution of their cybersecurity program. I believe we should encourage more institutions to deliver programs to train the security talent needed to adequately confront the cybersecurity challenge. We are only as strong as our weakest link and often the human component is that link. I believe there is also a need for more offensive security through hands-on penetration testing skillsets, requiring those to successfully attack and penetrate various live machines in a safe lab environment. In my opinion, we should be recruiting, educating, and training an army for this new frontier and the program here at DSU is one of many that should be filling that need in order to protect against an unseen attacker that can reside almost anywhere in the world, as long as there is an Internet connection.

In the absence of personnel, organizations can invest in a strong security infrastructure using often expensive hardware and software solutions. The gap, however, resides with the manpower to effectively implement, monitor and maintain such an infrastructure. There are a myriad of security-specific certifications available in the marketplace, many focus on security generalities and others are platform-specific. I believe there is also a need for more offensive security hands-on penetration testing skillsets, requiring those to successfully attack and penetrate various live machines in a safe lab environment. In my opinion, we should be recruiting, educating, and training an army for this new frontier and the program here at DSU is one of many that should be filling that need in order to protect against an unseen attacker that can reside almost anywhere in the world, as long as there is an Internet connection.

Frameworks = Roadmap

Industries often create or rely upon a standard for securing data, whether it be critical internal data, customer/patient information, intellectual property, trade secrets, financial data, and more. When we work with healthcare organizations, the Health Insurance Portability and Accountability Act (HIPAA) and Health Information Technology for Economic and Clinical Health Act (HITECH) are utilized as standards for ultimately securing patient health records. Financial institutions rely upon Federal Financial Institutions Examination Council (FFIEC) and Gramm-Leach-Bliley Act (GLBA) guidelines for securing customer information. Federal Government agencies and contractors thereto rely to varying degrees on the NIST Special Publication 800–53—Recommended Security Controls for Federal Information Systems. Cloud computing companies providing services to the Federal Government must comply with Federal Risk and Authorization Management Program (FedRAMP), and many Federal agencies and contractors must comply with Federal Information Systems Management Act (FISMA), both of which are based on NIST SP 800–53. Retailers and organizations processing, storing or transmitting credit/ debit card data utilize the Payment Card Industry (PCI) Data Security Standard (DSS). Some third party service providers will utilize the American Institution of Certified Public Accountants' (AICPA) Trust Services Principles for security, availability, processing integrity, confidentiality and privacy of data. Still others build information risk and security controls on an ISO 27000 or 31000 framework; or the Council on Cyber Security's 20 Critical Security Controls. These frameworks come in many shapes and sizes, ultimately with the same goal—protection and security of information. Yet it is very common for us to discuss NIST frameworks with IT staff, many with over 10 years experience, who are not familiar with those frameworks, what they provide, or how to use them.

There are a number of private and non-profit organizations that provide guidance on securing data. One such organization, HITRUST, is a collaboration of healthcare, business, technology and information security leaders. HITRUST has established the Common Security Framework (CSF), which is a framework that can be used by organizations, healthcare in particular, to secure personal health and financial information. The CSF is an information security framework that harmonizes the requirements of existing standards and regulations, including Federal (HIPAA, HITECH), third party (PCI, COBIT) and government (NIST, FTC).[5] In the same light, the Cloud Security Alliance (CSA) is an organization "dedicated to defining and raising awareness of best practices to help ensure a secure cloud computing environment. CSA harnesses the subject matter expertise of industry practitioners, associations, governments, and its corporate and individual members to offer cloud security-specific research, education, certification, events and products."[6] Other organizations, like the Multi-State Information Sharing Analysis Center,[7] the U.S. Chamber of Commerce,[8] and the Federal Trade Commission,[9] offer guides for assisting organizations with establishing a security environment designed to secure data. Many organizations have limited resources and others struggle with understanding their specific requirements and a direction for building a secure environment for protecting themselves, and ultimately their data, from cyber attacks. Most depend on their particular industry or their own customer requirements for guidance.

For organizations who are absent a regulated framework, the Council on Cyber Security's 20 Critical Security Controls are, in my opinion, an effective set of items that can be used across industries to build a control structure to combat against cyber threats. Consisting of the following, they provide organizations a much needed roadmap.

- Inventory of Authorized & Unauthorized Devices
- Inventory of Authorized & Unauthorized Software
- Secure Configurations for Hardware and Software on Mobile Devices, Laptops, Workstations, and Servers
- Continuous Vulnerability Assessment & Remediation
- Malware Defenses
- Application Software Security
- Wireless Access Control
- Data Recovery Capability
- Security Skills Assessment & Appropriate Training to Fill Gaps
- Secure Configurations for Network Devices such as Firewalls, Routers, and Switches
- Limitation and Control of Network Ports, Protocols and Services
- Controlled Use of Administration Privileges
- Boundary Defense
- Maintenance, Monitoring & Analysis of Audit Logs
- Controlled Access Based on the Need to Know
- Account Monitoring & Control
- Data Protection
- Incident Response and Management
- Secure Network Engineering

- Penetration Tests and Red Team Exercises

The key to effective implementation of these controls is the growth and development of a set of skilled resources in the marketplace.

I commend NIST, the Council on Cyber Security, HITRUST, FS–ISAC, and many other organizations, for creating security standards and guidelines for organizations to follow in order to protect themselves. I believe continued dialogue between industry groups and the legislative branch will help stress the importance of cybersecurity initiatives and further the understanding of security expectations in the marketplace.

Threat Intelligence

With cyber threats on the rise, I believe in the collaboration of public and private resources to share information about the attacks that are on the horizon. Cybersecurity by its nature is more reactive than proactive. Perpetrators are able to advance their tactics more rapidly than the defensive infrastructure. The "Deep Net" contains a number of forums offering free attack tools available to anyone with the goal of initiating any number of attack scenarios. An attacker can launch an attack at any time toward any target and the use of botnets make tracing the attack extremely difficult. The commercialization of malware tools also allows the hacking community to remain a step ahead. However, the more a specific type of attack occurs, the better the chance of recognizing it by collaboratively sharing threat intelligence. Network defense and incident response require a strong element of intelligence and counterintelligence that security teams must understand and leverage to successfully defend their cyber infrastructure, once again highlighting the need for an increase in technically qualified professionals.

The Department of Homeland Security is responsible for protecting our Nation's critical infrastructure from cyber threats and, according to its mission, information sharing is critical to create shared awareness of malicious cyber activity. The National Cybersecurity and Communications Integration Center (NCCIC) is a 24x7 cyber situational awareness, incident response, and management center for the Federal Government, intelligence community, and law enforcement. The Center shares information among the public and private sectors to provide greater understanding of cybersecurity and communications situation awareness of vulnerabilities, intrusions, incidents, mitigation, and recovery actions.

The Cyber Threat Intelligence Integration Center provides integrated all-source intelligence analysis related to foreign cyber threats and cyber incidents affecting U.S. national interests; support the U.S. government centers responsible for cybersecurity and network defense; and facilitate and support efforts by the government to counter foreign cyber threats.

Public-private partnerships like National Cybersecurity Alliance, HITRUST, FS–ISAC and others provide industry-specific resources for cyber and physical threat intelligence analysis and sharing. Forums like BlackHat and Defcon also provide valuable insight into emerging threats and how to combat them. I encourage the continued evolution of the sharing of threat intelligence between the public and private sectors.

Legislation

For the record, I do not believe additional regulation is necessary. Government has taken notice of the cybersecurity as challenges evidenced by the volume of recent legislation impacting cybersecurity. Recent legislation includes:

  P.L. 113–274, Cybersecurity Enhancement Act of 2014

  P.L. 113–282, National Cybersecurity Protection Act of 2014,

  P.L. 113–246, Cybersecurity Workforce Assessment Act

  H.R. 104, Cyber Privacy Fortification Act of 2015

  H.R. 234, Cyber Intelligence Sharing and Protection Act

  H.R. 555, Federal Exchange Data Breach Notification Act of 2015

  H.R. 580, Data Accountability and Trust Act

  H.R. 1053, Commercial Privacy Bill of Rights Act of 2015

  H.R. 1560, Protecting Cyber Networks Act

  H.R. 1704, Personal Data Notification and Protection Act of 2015

  H.R. 1731, National Cybersecurity Protection Advancement Act of 2015

  H.R. 1770, Data Security and Breach Notification Act of 2015

  H.R. 2205, Data Security Act of 2015

  S. 135, Secure Data Act of 2015

S. 177, Data Security and Breach Notification Act of 2015

S. 456, Cyberthreat Sharing Act of 2015

S. 547, Commercial Privacy Bill of Rights Act of 2015

S. 754, Cybersecurity Information Sharing Act of 2015

S. 961, Data Security Act of 2015

S. 1027, Data Breach Notification and Punishing Cyber Criminals Act of 2015

S. 1158, Consumer Privacy Protection Act of 2015

Bills like H.R. 1770 cite requirements for information security as follows: *"A covered entity shall implement and maintain reasonable security measures and practices to protect and secure personal information in electronic form against unauthorized access as appropriate for the size and complexity of such covered entity and the nature and scope of its activities."* Given the number of security frameworks available, as cited previously, it is apparent that guidance for "reasonable security measures" has been established. I believe other economic incentives will generate additional results. Evidence suggests that contractual implications are driving adherence to standards. Many organizations are being asked to demonstrate the effectiveness of their security controls as part of initiating a contract with a customer. Other economic incentives for the demonstration of "meaningful use" of a cybersecurity framework could prove valuable.

In addition to legislation, litigation is also a factor driving the necessity for more attention to cybersecurity controls. On August 24, a Third Circuit U.S. Court of Appeals panel of judges upheld the FTC's authority to play a key role in regulating cybersecurity relative to consumer data protection against breaches and allowed the FTC to proceed with a lawsuit against a large hotel chain citing "unfair business practice provisions" when it took inadequate security measures to protect consumer data after a breach that exposed over 600,000 payment cards. Litigation like this and a recent Neiman Marcus case, where 7th Circuit Court of Appeals reinstated a lawsuit against them over a 2013 data breach in which hackers stole credit card information from as many as 350,000 customers, could open a virtual Pandora's Box and pave the way for an unending line of class-action lawsuits that could change the economic landscape.

Conclusion

Thank you again for the opportunity to appear before you today to discuss our efforts to confront the challenges of cybersecurity. In conclusion, I highlight four areas that I believe need increased attention in order to combat cybersecurity challenges: a culture of security, the lack of skilled resources, a common framework, threat intelligence and the education, implementation and collaboration thereof.

Foster the Change to a Security Culture

I believe our society needs to experience a cultural shift in the attitude of security consciousness. Organizationally, culture is driven from the top of the organization, in boardrooms, C-suites, and executive management. Public/private sector collaboration should focus on education of businesses and consumers to increase awareness of evolving cyber threats and practices necessary to combat them. There are numerous examples of this effort, one of which is STOP.THINK.CONNECT by the National Cyber Security Alliance and the Department of Homeland Security. Regulated industries like healthcare, government and financial services have provided consumer education as part of mandated efforts.

Emphasis on Increasing Security Personnel

I believe we should invest further in developing programs for educating and training a section of the workforce to adequately address the ever-changing cyber threat landscape. We necessarily invest hundreds of billions of dollars in a military to protect our country and we need to be equipping and training a new "soldier" to protect both public and private entities in this evolving frontier. Programs like those at Dakota State University are leading the way.

Encourage Implementation of a Framework

I believe in the continued evolution of various frameworks, across industries, working to incorporate critical controls that are relevant to combat cybersecurity threats and encourage the implementation of the relative frameworks with the goal of reaching every organizations that handles a consumer's sensitive data.

Threat Intelligence Collaboration

I believe that collaborated information sharing between government agencies and the private sector is essential to confronting the challenges of cybersecurity. I encourage expanded private sector access to threat and intelligence from Federal intelligence and law enforcement agencies. The goal should be to provide organizations, including their third party vendors with information on threats, vulnerabilities, and exploits. The public sector should continue to coordinate information sharing efforts with industry organizations and others, like National Cybersecurity Alliance, HITRUST, FS–ISAC, and others.

Thank you again for this opportunity to present this testimony and I look forward to your questions.

Notes

1—"Data Breach Reports." *Identity Theft Resource Center* (n.d.): n. pag. 25 Aug. 2015. Web. 28 Aug. 2015. *<http://www.idtheftcenter.org/images/breach/DataBreachReports_2015.pdf>*.

2—"2015 Data Breach Investigations Report (DBIR)." *Verizon Enterprise Solutions.* Verizon, n.d. Web. 28 Aug. 2015. *<http://www.verizonenterprise.com/DBIR/2015/>*.

3—Torres, Alissa. "Maturing and Specializing: Incident Response Capabilities Needed." (August 2015): n. pag. *Https://www.sans.org/.* SANS Institute. Web. 28 Aug. 2015. *<https://www.sans.org/reading-room/whitepapers/analyst/maturing-specializing-incident-response-capabilities-needed_36162.pdf>*.

4—Richards, Kathleen. "Cybersecurity Skills Shortage Demands New Workforce Strategies." *SearchSecurity.* N.p., Aug. 2015. Web. 28 Aug. 2015. *<http://searchsecurity.techtarget.com/feature/Cybersecurity-skills-shortage-demands-new-workforce-strategies>*.

5—"About Us—HITRUST." *Hitrust About Us Comments.* N.p., 23 Jan. 2014. Web. 28 Aug. 2015. *<https://hitrustalliance.net/about-us/>*.

6—*About: Cloud Security Alliance.* N.p., n.d. Web. 28 Aug. 2015. *<https://cloudsecurity alliance.org/about/>*.

7—*Cyber Security: Getting Started: A Non Technical Guide.* Ely, Cambridgeshire, United Kingdom: It Governance, 2013. Multi-State Information Sharing & Analysis Center. Web. 28 Aug. 2015. *<https://msisac.cisecurity.org/resources/guides/documents/Getting_Started_Print .pdf>*.

8—"Internet Security Essentials for Business 2.0." (2012): n. pag. U.S. Chamber of Commerce. Web. 28 Aug. 2015. *<https://www.uschamber.com/sites/default/files/issues/technology/files/ ISEB–2.0-CyberSecurityGuide.pdf>*.

9—*Start with Security: A Guide for Business* (June 2015): n. pag. Federal Trade Commission. Web. 28 Aug. 2015. *<https://www.ftc.gov/system/files/documents/plain-language/pdf0205- start withsecurity.pdf>*.

The CHAIRMAN. Thank you, Mr. Pulse.

We turn now to Dr. Kevin Streff.

STATEMENT OF DR. KEVIN F. STREFF, DAKOTA STATE UNIVERSITY, FACULTY AND DEPARTMENT CHAIR—CYBER OPERATIONS AND SECURITY; FACULTY, UNIVERSITY OF WISCONSIN, GRADUATE SCHOOL OF BANKING; FOUNDER AND MANAGING PARTNER, SECURE BANKING SOLUTIONS, LLC; AND FOUNDER MANAGING PARTNER, HELIX SECURITY, LLC

Dr. STREFF. Chairman Thune and Ranking Member Nelson, members of the Senate Committee on Commerce, Science, and Transportation, I am very pleased to be here before you today on behalf of Dakota State University to share our views on the current state of cybersecurity readiness. DSU thanks you personally for your leadership on this issue.

There are 321 million Americans. It has been reported that over 850 million data records have been breached over the last 10 years. Cyber attacks occur daily on our networks, carrying out electronic crimes and disrupting our nation's digital infrastructure that Americans depend upon. Technology is simply advancing faster than our ability to secure it.

Further, two trends are making cybersecurity even more challenging over the coming decade. You mentioned one, the Internet of Things. The Internet of Things is an environment where everything is Internet-enabled—objects, animals, people, cars, dogs, refrigerators. In the 45 years of the Internet, it boasts 10 billion connections, and, as you mentioned, in the next 5 years, that is growing to 50 billion connections.

Couple that with the second trend, digital currency, which nobody has talked about here today. Bitcoin and other digital currencies are radically changing the face of money exchange. It is a new way of exchanging value. Coupled with the Internet of Things, this seems like the perfect storm for cyber criminals to wreak havoc on our electric systems like we have never seen before.

Some additional areas of concern: America's national cybersecurity strategy was last updated in 2003. Small businesses and medium businesses often lack the resources and knowledge to deal with cyber threats. Mark mentioned a twist-tie company attacked out of Brazil.

Data-breach notification is inconsistent in 48 states, and I know that Congress is taking that issue up, hopefully.

Cybersecurity risk management practices are insufficient. This leads to a lack of metrics and a lack of measurement in the space. And that is what Eric was getting to with his testimony.

The lack of security awareness may be our number-one issue. Clicking on things, opening things, sharing things, installing things—these are major training issues that have to get addressed.

And, finally, as everybody is talking about, there is a national shortage of security experts. Symantec, the world's largest software security vendor, recently reported that the demand for a cybersecurity workforce is expected to rise by 6 million professionals globally by 2019, leaving us with a projected shortfall of 1.5 million cybersecurity professionals. According to CIO Magazine, cybersecurity professionals today report an average salary of $116,000.

SBS people, don't pay any attention to that.

[Laughter.]

Dr. STREFF. Items for the Committee and yourself to consider, Chairman: We would encourage you to pass the Cybersecurity Information Sharing Act of 2015 and to take up that Federal data-breach notification law.

Second, we would like to see you work to update and maintain the national cybersecurity strategy that has goals, objectives, funding sources. And might we suggest that, while there are 20 infrastructures that are identified as critical infrastructures, might we look at power and telecommunications as two infrastructures that are even more critical than others, that banking, health care, and everything depends upon.

Third, improving grant opportunities and funding for research in cybersecurity, with an emphasis on risk management practices, metrics and measurements, and security awareness solutions.

And, finally, expanding our cybersecurity workforce and improving cybersecurity training, building upon the NSA/DHS Centers of Excellence program with more scholarships, financial support, to make this an even more attractive field so that cybersecurity becomes a career choice and we can address that million-jobs job shortage.

In conclusion, the risk to our Nation is clear that a cyber terrorist thousands of miles away can hold a citizen, country, or organization hostage with binary attacks. We need a cybersecurity strategy that focuses our resources, promotes awareness, training, and education for business leaders and consumers, promotes information-sharing and customer notification, and builds that cybersecurity workforce of tomorrow.

To Chairman Thune and the Committee, thank you for the opportunity to participate in this important and timely hearing. DSU looks forward to working with all stakeholders to improve the security of the electronic infrastructure all businesses in America use.

[The prepared statement of Dr. Streff follows:]

PREPARED STATEMENT OF DR. KEVIN F. STREFF, DAKOTA STATE UNIVERSITY, FACULTY AND DEPARTMENT CHAIR—CYBER OPERATIONS AND SECURITY; FACULTY—UNIVERSITY OF WISCONSIN, GRADUATE SCHOOL OF BANKING; FOUNDER AND MANAGING PARTNER—SECURE BANKING SOLUTIONS, LLC; FOUNDER AND MANAGING PARTNER—HELIX SECURITY, LLC

Witness Statement

Kevin Streff, Ph.D. is an Associate Professor and Department Chair at Dakota State University in Madison, SD and conducts cybersecurity education and research in the financial services sector, with a particular focus on understanding the security issues of small and medium-sized financial institutions. Dr. Streff works with the banking associations all across the United States to understand rural banking vulnerabilities and solutions to mitigate. Dr. Streff has over 25 years of experience working in insurance, banking and credit operations.

Professor Streff teaches managerial elements of information security, including risk management, security policy, information security management systems, disaster recovery, business continuity planning, auditing, and incident response planning. Dr. Streff has numerous publications in peer-reviewed journals such *Journal of Information Warfare, Journal of Computer Information Systems, Journal of Autonomic and Trusted Computing Journal of Computing Sciences in Colleges,* and *Issues in Information Systems.* He is the recipient of over $7.5 million in grants and contracts over the past ten years. Dr. Streff serves on several conference program committees, including International Conference on Information Warfare, and Cybersecurity, Network, Database and Software Security. Dr. Streff was session chair at several prestigious systems science conferences over the past several years, including organizing and chairing a mini-track on Information on Information Assurance and Computer Security at the International Conference on Information Warfare. Dr. Streff was a keynote speaker at several national security conferences, presented over two hundred times at state, regional and national banking conferences, and published in both America's Banker and Community Banker. He has been featured on *ABC News, Forbes Magazine* and *National Public Radio.*

Dr. Streff is Founder of Dakota State's security program, and currently serves as Department Chair for the Cyber Operations and Security department, which has been recognized by The Department of Homeland Security and The National Security Agency as a Center of Excellence in Information Security Education, Research and Cyber Operations. He is also Founder and Past-President of InfraGard South Dakota, an FBI outreach program to promote the protection of critical infrastructure in SD, ND and MN. He is also Founder and Past-President of Secure Banking Solutions, an information security consulting firm focused on improving information security in community banks and cred it unions in the U.S. SBS assists over 900 small and medium-sized financial institutions in 48 states with their information security and compliance needs. Dr. Streff is on faculty at the Graduate School of Banking at the University of Wisconsin where he helped develop the recently launched Bank Technology Management School and Bank Security School.

Introduction

Chairman Thune, Ranking Member Nelson and Members of the Senate Committee on Commerce, Science, and Transportation, I am pleased to appear before you today on behalf of Dakota State University to share our views on the current state of data/cybersecurity. These comments will be made address our countries readiness to identify and thwart attacks on businesses and our Nation's critical electronic infrastructure. Particular emphasis will be placed upon small business security and the cybersecurity readiness level of the banking sector.

My name is Dr. Kevin Streff and I am Department Chair of the Cyber Operations and Security Program at Dakota State University which has been recognized by The

Department of Homeland Security and The National Security Agency as a Center of Excellence in Information Security Education, Research and Cyber Operations. Along with Dr. Pauli, I am here today representing one of the top cybersecurity programs in the Nation. We appreciate the invitation to appear before the committee on this important issue, and thank the committee for their leadership and foresight in dealing with these issues before a crisis state.

Background

Systematic and repeated cyberattacks occur daily against our defense, government, academic, and industry networks looking to carry out a variety of electronic crime and disruption of our Nation's digital infrastructure. In 1998, Presidential Decision Directive 63 identified 18 critical infrastructures, which America depends upon daily. Are we prepared to handle a digital attack against our cyber infrastructure? 4.5 million small and medium-sized businesses are also under heavy attack and constitute substantial risk of loss to our economy. In fact, most small and medium-sized business lack the requisite skills and resources to combat these cyber threats.

In this testimony, we will review the current legal and regulatory environment in which financial institutions and small and medium-sized businesses must operate (SECTION I), communicate technology trends to consider (SECTION II), discuss security and privacy experiences in the financial services sector that have impacted small and medium-sized financial institutions (SECTION III), and discuss cybersecurity concerns and recommendations for the President and Commerce Committee to consider (SECTION IV).

Section I. Overview of Current Data Protection Laws, Regulation, and Policy Statements in Financial Services

A. 1970—Bank Secrecy Act

In 1970, Congress passed the Bank Secrecy Act (BSA). BSA requires U.S. financial institutions to assist U.S. government agencies to detect and prevent money laundering. The act specifically requires financial institutions to keep records of cash purchases of negotiable instruments, file reports of cash transactions exceedingly daily aggregate amount of $10,000, and to report suspicious activity that might signify money laundering, tax evasion, or other criminal activities. Several anti-money laundering acts, including provisions in title III of the USA PATRIOT Act, have been enacted up to the present to amend the BSA. (See 31USC 5311–5330 and 31 CFR Chapter X (formerly 31CFR Part 103). The documents filed by financial institutions under BSA are used by law enforcement agencies, both domestic and international to identify, detect and deter money laundering whether it is in furtherance of a criminal enterprise, terrorism, tax evasion or other unlawful activity.

B. 1999—Financial Industries Modernization Act of 1999 (Gramm-Leach-Bliley)

The Gramm-Leach-Bliley Act (GLBA) 15 U.S.C. §§ 6801–6810 (disclosure of personal financial information), 15 U.S.C. §§ 6821–6827 (fraudulent access) repealed the GlassSteagall Act of 1932, and is part of broader legislation which removes barriers to banks engaging in a wider scope of financial services. GLBA applies to financial institutions use and disclosure of non-public financial information about consumers. Section 501(b) requires administrative, technical, and physical safeguards to protect covered non-public personal information. Federal banking agencies have published Interagency Guidelines Establishing Standards for Information Security for financial institutions subject to their jurisdiction. 66 Fed. Reg. 8616 (February 1, 2001) and 69 Fed. Reg. 77610 (December 28, 2004). The Guidelines are published by each agency in the Code of Federal Regulations, including:

- Federal Deposit Insurance Corporation, 12 C.F.R., Part 364, App. B;
- Office of the Comptroller of the Currency, 12 C.F.R., Part 30, App. B;
- Board of Governors of the Federal Reserve System, 12 C.F.R., Part 208, App. D–2 and Part 225, App. F;
- Office of Thrift Supervision, 12 C.F.R., Part 570, App. B; and
- National Credit Union Administration, 12 C.F.R., Part 748

The Federal Trade Commission has issued a final rule, Standards for Safeguarding Customer Information, 16 C.F.R. Part 314, and the Securities and Exchange Commission promulgated Regulation S–P: Privacy of Consumer Financial Information, 17 C.F.R. Part 248 for financial institutions within their respective jurisdictions. These requirements mean that all financial institutions must develop, document and operationalize a comprehensive information security program. The administrative, technical and physical safeguards are sweeping and expansively interpreted by Federal and state regulators to include everything from the physical security of buildings, data security at service providers, to the types of authentication used during online banking sessions. Each bank must report annually to the Board of Directors on the status of the information security program. The Guidelines require a risk assessment designed to: "identify reasonably foreseeable internal and external threats" to customer information, assess the likelihood and potential damage of these threats, and to assess the effectiveness of a wide variety of information security controls. GLBA is significant because of the extensive requirements and regulatory oversight imposed upon the financial industry and carried out by Federal and state regulators.

C. 2001—USA PATRIOT Act

The USA PATRIOT (Patriot Act), enacted by President George W. Bush in 2001, reduced restrictions on law enforcement agencies' ability to search telephone, e-mail communications, medical, financial, and other records; eased restrictions on foreign intelligence gathering within the United States; expanded the Secretary of the Treasury's authority to regulate financial transactions. Section 314(b) of the USA PATRIOT Act permits financial institutions, upon providing notice to the U.S. Department of the Treasury, to share information with one another in order to identify and report to the Federal Government activities that may involve money laundering or terrorist activity. More specifically, the BSA authorizes the Treasury to require financial institutions to maintain records of personal financial transactions that "have a high degree of usefulness in criminal, tax and regulatory investigations and proceedings" and to report "suspicious transaction relevant to a possible violation of law or regulation." Again, because The Patriot Act deals with governmental, rather than private, intrusion into customer privacy, it is outside the scope of this discussion.

D. 2002—Sarbanes Oxley Act

The Sarbanes-Oxley Act of 2002 (SOX) was enacted to restore confidence in the integrity of the financial reporting process at publicly traded companies, influenced by high profile accounting scandals at firms such as Enron and WorldCom. However, each publically-traded financial institution that is affected by the Sarbanes-Oxley Act has some level of reliance on automated information systems to process, store and transact the data that is the basis of financial reports, and SOX requires financial institutions to consider the IT security controls that are in place to promote the confidentiality, integrity, and accuracy of this data. SOX states that specific attention should be given to the controls that act to secure the corporate network, prevent unauthorized access to systems and data, and ensure data integrity and availability in the case of a disaster or other disruption of service. Also, each system that interfaces with critical financial reporting data should have validation controls such as edit and limit checks built-into further minimize the likelihood of data inaccuracy.

E. 2006—Payment Card Industry Standard

The Payment Card Industry Security Standards Council is an Industry group formed to manage and maintain the Data Security Standard (DSS), which was created by the Council to ensure the security of payment card information. Sensitive data is involved in card transactions, including account number, cardholder name, expiration date, and PIN. The intent of the PCI DSS is to ensure that card transactions occurring across multiple private and public networks are subject to end-to-end transaction security. The payment card industry consists of Card Issuers, Card Holders, Merchants, Acquirers, and Card Associations. From the collection of card information at a point of sale, transmission through the merchant's systems to the acquiring bank's systems, then on to the card issuer, the PCI DSS requirements attempt to ensure sufficient security safeguards are in place on the card data from beginning to the end of a card transaction. Enforcement of the security requirements is done by the card associations and through a certification process of each association member. The certification process is carried out by Qualified Security Assessors (QSA) who audit systems and networks to ensure the mandatory controls are in place. Certification does not guarantee that an organization will not suffer a data breach, as several PCI certified organizations have suffered data breach incidents.

F. 2013—Identify Theft Red Flags Rule

The Identify Theft Red Flags Rule (Red Flags Rule) requires financial institutions to implement a written Identity Theft Prevention Program that is designed to detect the warning signs of identity theft in their daily operations. By identifying red flags in advance, financial institutions will be better able to identify suspicious patterns that may arise, and take steps to prevent a red flag from escalating into identity theft.

A financial institution Identity Theft Red Flags Program should enable the organization to:

1. Identify relevant patterns, practices, and specific forms of activity—the "red flags"—that signal possible identity theft;
2. Incorporate business practices to detect red flags;
3. Detail appropriate response to any red flags you detect to prevent and mitigate identity theft; and
4. Be updated periodically to reflect changes in risk from identity theft.

Shortly thereafter, regulatory agencies began issuing examination procedures to assist financial institutions in implementing the Identity Theft Red Flags, Address Discrepancies, and Change of Address Regulations, reflecting the requirements of Sections 114 and 315 of the Fair and Accurate Credit Transaction s Act of 2003.

G. 2015 Cyber Security Guidance

The recent focus of the bank examiners has been cybersecurity readiness. In fact, in 2013 and 2014, FFIEC conducted a 500 bank study to examine the preparedness level of the U.S. banking system and documented their findings which included some major shortcomings, especially in the risk management, awareness, information sharing and leadership domains. They subsequently documented a cybersecurity risk-based approach which most banks are examining as we speak to determine next steps. The study also focused on the Board and management team being able to set "the tone at the top" as it relates to cybersecurity.

H. Miscellaneous Regulatory Guidance

The Federal Financial Institutions Examination Council (FFIEC) is a formal interagency body empowered to prescribe uniform principles, standards, and report forms for the Federal examination of financial institutions by the Federal financial regulatory agencies." As such, the FFIEC publishes the "Information Technology Examination Handbook", which is used by banking regulators in executing examinations of information technology and systems of financial institutions. The Hand book includes ten (10) booklets, one of which is the "Information Security Booklet", which provides a baseline against which a financial institution subject to GLBA can be evaluated. The "Information Security Booklet" attempts to provide a high level, comprehensive overview of the major types of information security controls one would necessarily expect to be operating effectively with in a financial institution. The types of controls are not limited in applicability to just financial institutions, and are derived from the same principles underpinning all major in formation security frameworks.

I. Third Party Self-Regulation

Small and medium-sized financial institutions depend heavily on hardware and software vendors for nearly all banking products. In addition, many of these vendors become service providers offering to host and manage their products for the small and medium-sized financial institution (SMFI). The service provider industry has experienced several significant data breaches affecting the financial services industry in the past several years, including Target (40 million data records), JP Morgan Chase (71.5 million data records), Office of Personnel Management (21.5 million data records), UCLA Health System (4.5 million data records), etc. When companies choose to outsource data processing to a third party, they typically perform information security due diligence on the third party to understand how the data will be protected. A very common standard for third party assurance has been the SSAE16 standard. BITS, a non-profit organization, has also attempted to standardize the assessment of third-party service providers by developing the "BITS Framework for Managing Technology Risk for Service Provider Relationships", which includes two tools to help service providers in control selection and implementation. In summary, SMFIs operate in an increasingly complex regulatory environment, with community banks regulated aggressively and credit unions a little less. This regulation is necessary, but causes significant financial, resource, and other issues in SMFIs who must leverage technology to compete. Increasing regulation is likely as additional technologies are deployed and the cybersecurity stakes grow, but all increased regulation must be tempered with a SMFI's ability to stay in business and meet the needs of their customers. The majorities of SMFI's are in rural locations and may be the only local funding source for a community.

Section II. Technology Trends

Technology is advancing faster than SMFIs' ability to respond with appropriate mitigating security controls. For example, the use of cell phone cameras to take a picture of a check as the basis for making an electronic deposit into an account, or P2P payment transactions by cell phones create security exposures for which there are inadequate controls to prevent fraud. Fortunately, most SMFIs are not first adopters of new technology, but rather prefer to wait until the systems become more seasoned before embracing newer technologies. Moreover, the timeline between introduction, implementation and adoption of new technology by consumers continues to shrink. Just ten years ago, data processing was the buzz where computers were essentially back-off equipment designed to promote efficiency in the financial institution. Today, technology is front-line differentiators for banks and businesses, with customers demanding to use mobile technologies and social media to conduct commerce. The risk profile ten years ago included someone breaking into the bank's computer to get customer records, while the risk profile today is someone breaking in to cell phones, laptops, mobile devices, social media sites, merchants who deposit checks via imaging systems, service providers who host critical banking applications, websites which validate flood plains or credit bureau information, etc. This list goes on and on regarding the technologies typical in a SMFI. The next generation of technologies will exponentially increase the risk profile because information and Infrastructure will be further distributed, and not partitioned off by the walls of the bank. With the increase in outsourcing and the mounting risks of offshoring, requiring data centers to be located in the U.S. seems consistent with the goal of increasing our cybersecurity posture. Banks leverage Brinks trucks to secure the delivery of cash to their bank. The financial industry needs to devise "cyber Brinks trucks" to perform the same role in cyberspace.

Two major trends will likely drive technology and security over the coming decade. First, the Internet of Things (IoT) is an environment in which objects, animals or people are provided with unique identifiers and the ability to transfer data over a network without requiring human-to-human or human-to-computer interaction. IoT has evolved from the convergence of wireless technologies, micro-electro-mechanical systems and the Internet. By 2020, there will be a quarter billion connected vehicles on the road, enabling new in-vehicle services and automated driving capabilities, according to Gartner. All cities will (eventually) be smart. With more than one-half of the world's population living in cities, innovative new IoT solutions, such as smart parking, connected waste, and traffic management, hold great promise for combatting the major challenges of rapid urbanization. We are unlikely to see many smart cities of the future appearing overnight. However, like in the past with the adoption of revolutionary technologies such as sewers, electricity, traffic lights, and the Internet, mayors will slowly implement IoT solutions to save money, shape the future and make their cities better places to live. We will be trading mobile dollars for IoT pennies. It is no wonder that the mobile operators are salivating at the prospect of a windfall of new revenue to be earned from connecting the projected 50 billion devices, or things, to the Internet (today there are approximately 10 billion things connected to the Internet). However, it is not that straight forward. While some of the traffic will flow over mobile networks, the majority of the connections will be made over wireline or unlicensed wireless networks. And, many of the IOT devices require very low bandwidth—simply conveying their status on an occasional basis and then remaining dormant until this status changes. Mobile operators will need to do more than just sell mobile connectivity to inanimate objects to reap the full rewards of IoT. It will be about much more than the "things". The currency of IoT will be "data". But, this new currency only has value if the masses of data can be translated into insights and information which can be converted into concrete actions that will transform businesses, change people's lives and effect social change.

The second major trend is digital currency. While no digital currency will soon dislodge the dollar, bitcoin (and other digital currencies) are much more than a currency. It is a radically new, decentralized system for managing the way societies exchange value. It is, quite simply, one of the most powerful innovations in finance in 500 years. It's already proven that bitcoin has contributed a lot to the world. For example, PayPal recently urged everyone to use digital currencies in their transactions and predicted that these currencies will be accepted by the majority of the population and establishments in the U.S. within 12 months. However, the shadowy fact remains that bitcoins and digital currencies have been risky. Frustrations have mounted when the price of the Bitcoin came crashing down. Mt. Gox closing down, China banning their use, laws provided by states against it and more—these all contributed to the gradual decline of bitcoins popularity and price value. The number of attacks involving Bitcoin mining malware tripled: from 360,065 attacks in 2013 to 1,204,987 in 2014. But the reality is these digital currencies are in their infancy and the issues of today will get solved for mass acceptance and use in our economy. Put together with the Internet of Things where 50 billion devices will be connected to the Internet by 2020, it is easy to see how digital currencies could be deployed as the backbone currency in the digital age.

Section III. Data Security and Privacy Issues in the Financial Sector and Small Businesses

Over 850 million data records have been breached over the past ten years:

857,702,257 Records in our database from 4584 Breaches made public fitting this criteria
Source: PrivacyRights.Org

How many of these data records and breaches involved the *financial sector*?

349,188,179 Records in our database from 608 Breaches made public fitting this criteria
Source: PrivacyRights.Org

How many of these data records and breaches involved the *retail sector*?

257,514,157 Records in our database from 547 Breaches made public fitting this criteria
Source: PrivacyRights.Org

Note that these numbers are likely dramatically understated as universal notification laws are not in place and punishment for not disclosing is often not a deterrent. For example, JP Morgan Chase breach is not accounted for on this site. The breach numbers are likely a fraction of the actual activity that is occurring. It is also interesting to note that healthcare and government (which receive much security attention) have fewer breaches that small businesses and/or retail. Claims that the PCI standard are sufficient seem to be overstated as retail accounts for the highest percentage of data records breached in 2014.

U.S. SMFIs and small and medium-sized entities (SMEs) are important as millions of consumers depend upon community banks, credit unions, accounting firms, tax-preparation firms, investment offices, insurance agencies, and the like. When issues in the financial system exist, confidence erodes and consumers are left paralyzed wondering what to do. The margin for error in SMEs is relatively small, and one such data breach can shut the doors on viable businesses.

Further, if terrorists would target these vulnerable SMFIs or SMEs, they would find a soft underbelly of relatively under-protected targets. A plethora of nefarious activities are then possible, including stealing and selling customer data, extorting ransoms, "owning" the computer, making these systems unavailable, etc. Stated directly, these activities could be enough to put a SME or SMFI out of business. The reality is that while it is nearly impossible to challenge the importance of SMEs and SMFIs in the U.S., it is equally difficult to convince security experts that either are prepared to protect their critical systems, important customer information and do their part to battle against the war on terror.

The Federal Government identified banking and finance as a critical infrastructure that requires protection, yet most of the attention is paid to the large financial institutions. SMFIs and SMEs store and transmit much non-public data, with limited resources to fend off a well-equipped, well-funded enemy. A recent survey of bank executives called out this very fact. When asked what their top technology concern was over the next two years, risk management and compliance topped the list. A black market drives insiders and hackers to steal information because of its value. Nine out of ten data breaches could be easily avoided with basic preventative controls consistently applied. SMFIs and SMEs have a wealth of nonpublic, sensitive data that cyber thieves are targeting with increasing regularity.

Cyber security is a broad and pervasive issue leading to at least two national issues: critical information protection and identify theft. Critical information protection is guarding our electronic infrastructures as an issue of national security. Incidents are classified, but it is well established that China and others are interested in technology disruptions that affect the United States' ability to conduct commerce. President Obama is on record stating that the United States is not prepared for critical infrastructure protection (CIP) and despite national budget pressures is created in 2013 a division within the national government (U.S. Cyber Command) to begin focusing on this new national issue.

Identity theft remains a fast growing crime in America and the risks of not protecting such information can be catastrophic to SMEs in communities. When identities of good U.S. citizens are stolen by cyber criminals, the good citizen can be humiliated, lack good credit, and spend significant time and money in an attempt to partially restore their good name. Information risk management is the first step in resolving the broad and pervasive issues of CIP and Identity Theft. Public Law 111–24 was signed by the President establishing a Small Business Information Security Task Force to look in to the issue.

The Ponemon Institute, an independent research firm which conducts research on privacy, data protection and cybersecurity, calculates in 2014 businesses paid an average of $230 per compromised record. Consequently, for a small company with 500 compromised customer records, this would math to $115,000. Companies may keep inactive customers in their database as well, magnifying the number of customers impacted and the resources to manage thru a breach. Simply said, a data breach can be so costly that it can put a company out of business or halt expansion plans. This issue is amplified in America where there is very limited information security expertise, offering unprotected businesses as easy targets for organized cyber criminals with financial motivation.

Electronic Crimes in Commercial Banking with Small and Medium-Sized Financial Institutions

Organized cyber-gangs are increasingly preying on small and medium-sized companies in the U.S., setting off a multi-million-dollar online crime wave and grave concerns that critical infrastructure government and business depends upon each day may become compromised. It appears there are three contributing reasons they are growing so fast: (1) Low threat of arrest in these "safe havens", (2) High payout for the crime, and (3) Victim sharing data on these attacks has been minimal. The attacks are amazingly simple and the amount of money taken, information stolen, or infrastructure compromised is concerning.' SMEs do not know how to protect themselves. In some cases where credit card theft has occurred, they have had to shut down because they lost the ability to process credit cards. Small businesses are being affected greatly by poor security practices. It is not a risk issue, but rather an issue of survival. Cyber criminals view SMEs as easy targets without the resources or knowledge to fend them off or prosecute them if caught. Consequently, cyber criminals are turning their attention to perceived easy targets in America. Identity thieves can cost SMFIs and SMEs their basic ability to stay in business (*i.e.*, financial losses, bad publicity of a data breach, significant costs of recovering from a data breach, inability to process credit cards, etc.). Even if there were no measurable damages to customers, the notification costs alone can put the SME out of business. One-third of companies said that a significant security breach could put their company out of business. Many SMEs are having a difficult time in this economy, and even the smallest of distractions can be devastating. SMFIs, too, are struggling with increased assessment fees, limited deposits, limited fee-based products, and overwhelming compliance expenses, which is spurring closures and consolidation in the industry.

While SMFIs have struggled to keep pace with hackers, the SMEs have clearly fallen short. In a study I completed of SMEs, 7 out of 10 SMEs lack at least one basic security control, such as a firewall, antivirus software, strong passwords, or basic security awareness for staff. Many SMEs simply lack the basic security most of us expect on our home PCs. As evidence, I provide a statistic. I am founder of Secure Banking Solutions, LLC, a security/privacy firm focused on information security and compliance for SMFIs. As such, SBS is regularly hired to conduct penetration tests on SMFIs where SBS security personnel run (after authorization) hacking tools to see if they can break into the bank's network and systems. SBS is effective in 24 percent of SMFIs (meaning that SBS personnel were able to gain access to Information and systems they were not authorized for). To contrast, SBS is effective in 100 percent of SME penetration tests. The question is "why?" and the answer is simple: SMFIs are regulated to a certain level of security that is far superior to a SME. Most anyone can download hacking tools from the Internet, point them at a SME, and gain unauthorized access, zombie the machine, steal data, or disrupt the environment.

Traditionally, most SMEs have viewed security as a problem faced solely by large organizations, government agencies, or online intensive operations as large organizations possess large, prolific information targets and are generally more regulated than SMEs. However, cyber criminals are finding easy targets in SMEs that have limited security. The financial gain for cyber thieves targeting SMEs is obviously less than that of large organizations, but they can be hacked in significantly less time with little to no effort. Tools to conduct these attacks on SMEs are freely downloadable from the Internet.

The FBI previously issued an alert to all SMFIs and SMEs of this issue. These attacks are working because of a lack of security controls at the SME whereby

41

fraudulent transactions are directly taken out of commercial customer's bank accounts. The current generation of banking products work because of technology, including remote deposit capture, Internet banking, mobile Banking, item imaging, and on-line account origination. However, USA Today quoted Amrit Williams, a chief technology officer, "Any organization that cannot survive a sudden five-or six-figure loss should consider shunning Internet banking altogether." Banking security analyst at Gartner, Avivah Litan, tells acquaintances that run small businesses to switch from commercial online accounts to an individual consumer account to take advantage of consumer-protection laws under Regulation E. Regulation E protection does not exist for corporate accounts; consequently, SMEs have no legal protection if commercial account fraud occurs. Unlike individual accounts that protect individual consumers to a maximum exposure of $50 if fraud occurs, corporate accounts have no such protection. The SME can sue or go to the media, but these approaches likely do not get the money back and drains even more resources from SME, which are typically resource challenged.

New fees levied by financial institutions on paper-based banking products are likely to push more small businesses in to banking online, whether or not they are aware of and prepared for the types of sophisticated cyber-attacks that have cost organizations tens of millions of dollars in recent months. Gartner analysts say banks should not be pushing more businesses into online banking without adequately informing them of the risks. The reality is that the perfect small-business storm is occurring: heaving attacks are already beginning and significantly more technology will be deployed by SMFIs over the next five years, creating a fertile cyber ground for terrorists to create problems.

The latest Business Banking Trust Study provides insights from the SME perspective on the pervasiveness of fraud, the state of security at banks and businesses, and the impact fraud has on businesses' relationships with their banks. The study found:

- 74 percent of businesses surveyed experienced online fraud;
- 52 percent of businesses reported experiencing payments fraud or attempted payments fraud in the last 12 months;
- In 72 percent of fraud cases, banks failed to catch fraud involving the illegal transfer of funds or other nefarious practices such as information identity theft; and
- 70 percent of SMEs have diminished confidence in their FI or take their banking business elsewhere.

More than nine out of ten small business owners in the study cited cybersecurity as a concern. This is not an unfounded fear: Half of them report they've already suffered a cyber-attack, with 61 percent of those attacks taking place in the last 12 months. The National Cyber Security Alliance conducted the National Small Business Security Study with Visa Inc. to analyze small business' cybersecurity practices and attitudes. Results include:

- 94 percent of small business owners report being very or somewhat concerned about cybersecurity; and
- Nearly half of businesses surveyed report they already have been a victim of a cyber-attack.

In summary, there is little doubt that the financial services sector is under attack for identity theft and infrastructure corruption motives. There is also little double that the small and medium-sized businesses and financial institutions are coming in the cross-hairs of cyber criminals. The number and significance of data breaches and attacks is significant, and only a comprehensive approach that looks at all infrastructure holistically (from government, academia, and industry) can ward off these terrorists.

Section IV. Observations and Recommendations

This section outlines several observations and summarizes recommendations to address cybersecurity as a nation, and in both banks and small businesses alike.

Concerns

1. Lack of a National Cyber Security Strategy—The lack of a comprehensive, bilaterally supported national security strategy is problematic at best. When the President and Congress is on record time and time again declaring the imminent danger the Internet represents, then shouldn't it follow that resources area aligned to this grave danger? The current administration seems to understand the magnitude of the issue but has been remiss to draft a com-

prehensive strategy to lead our digital infrastructure into a more secure future.

2. Internet of Things and Digital Currencies will Accelerate Internet Traffic and Growth—It is fair to say that we cannot manage the Internet environment of today with 10 billion connections and an architecture that doesn't scale well. It took nearly 45 years to get to these 10 billion connection; yet, by the end of 2020 the Internet will include 50 billion connection. Add to this the use of digital monies (*i.e.,* bitcoin) to settle the transactions and this seems like a perfect storm where cyber criminals will wreak havoc on our electronic systems like we have never seen before. Refer to Appendix A and B for Internet and Internet of Things growth statistics.

3. Cyber War (or Cyber in War) is Imminent—The power grid represents tremendous risk to American citizens as aggressive nation states continue to ready to attack our SCADA infrastructures. While it is foreseeable that a multi-variant attack coordinated across sector to simultaneously interfere with power, telecommunications, oil/gas and banking infrastructure is plausible, more likely is a single deep rooted attack on a single infrastructure to ingest cyber terror into our citizens' conscious. It is also plausible that cyber war will lead to kinetic war (or some combination of the two). Specifically, an offensive attack by a nation on our power infrastructure could be met with a kinetic attack on their nation's physical target (or vice versa).

4. Banking Continues to be the Most Attacked Sector—Based upon volume (number of data records, number of attacks, etc.), the financial sector continues to be the most attacked of our infrastructures. The interconnected nature of this sector has caused the banking regulators to become very concerned about vendor management and corporate account takeover. With the growth of Internet of Things, it is possible that there could be a shift in attention from the hackers; however, it is fair to say that banking and financial services are under attack today and this will likely continue over the next five to ten years.

5. Small Business Security Continue to Lag Behind—Small businesses lack the resources to understand and mitigate these cyber threats. The PCI standards are clearly not working, and for the most part based on voluntary compliance and self-audit. Today, the best mitigation strategy seems to be to educate individuals and SMEs to the risks and controls that are essential to minimize the potential for major cyber loss or disruption. Moreover, we do not think it is appropriate or reasonable to shift the burden of loss from the person or organization that had inadequate controls in place to detect and deter cyber hacking attacks, to the financial institutions that process the withdrawals by the crooks, generally through ACH debits.

6. Information Sharing is Lacking but Improving—The ISACs were devised over ten years ago, yet it is really only this year that the FS–ISAC is gaining momentum. With the banking regulators getting behind FS–ISAC, banks and credit unions have increased membership rates. The system really only work if many are participating, and we are finally getting to a scale where there is value.

7. Data Breach Notification is Inconsistent—48 states have data breach notification laws; however, every state law is different. This lack of uniformity make it difficult to measure breach rates and makes it difficult for the consumer to understand what is going on.

8. Security Awareness (or the lack thereof) is the Number One Issue

   a. Citizens
   b. Business Owners
   c. Investors
   e. Policymakers
   d. Executives

   A recent study in the banking sector determine that the number one cybersecurity issue in banking is the reality that senior management and boards are simply not in position to establish "the tone from the top" as it relates to cybersecurity. The lack the requisite skills to set the direction and manage their organizations to achieve cybersecurity objectives.

9. The Internet of Today Can Not Be Secured—The Internet was not built for the purpose it carries out today. The Internet was not conceived to become the backbone for commerce. While today countries and companies alike are

adopting technologies to grow their interests, the Internet lacks fundamental controls that large-scale networks must have. As the Internet-of-Things explodes over the next ten years and our cyber adversaries grow in both number and strength, the problems of will seem like child's play. Infrastructures like the Internet takes years to change because of its pervasive and invasive nature. The time is now to determine how the infrastructure we know today must be secured and/or fundamentally changed so that cyber resources remain available, accurate and private to those who depend upon them for social and economic well-being.

10. Industry Will Continue to Underinvest in Cyber Security Solutions—Digital Infrastructure is Infrastructure. When an ice storm occurs in North Dakota, icing up power lines and taking out power, the region is paralyzed until power is restored. It can sometimes take weeks and months to complete this task, depending upon the tenacity of Mother Nature. What would happen to these financial institutions, our economy, and our consumer confidence level if malicious nation-states disrupted our power instead of an ice storm? How long would it take for power to be restored on power grid infrastructure dating back centuries? Power, water, transportation, and the Internet just to name a few are all required to conduct banking commerce. While SMFIs are required to devise business continuity, incident response, and pandemic prepared ness plans, no SMFI could operate if essential infrastructure we all depend up (such as the power grid) was compromised. The job is much larger than any one SMFI. To the degree major and minor changes are needed at SMFIs or SMEs, we urge the Administration to consider this infrastructure and fund it. There needs to be a mindset shift away from industry paying for everything in this infrastructure (because they created it and are the users of it) to some shared cost model. If this infrastructure is truly a matter of national security then the Federal Government has a funding responsibility. Just as tanks, planes, and weapons are funded to protect our interests, we urge the Administration to consider their financial responsibilities as it relates to this vital electronic infrastructure.

11. Securing Our Digital Infrastructure Will Take Cooperation and Resources— Nearly 20 critical infrastructures are identified and would take trillions of dollars to "secure". This resource allocation is likely unreasonable so little will be done to remarkably improve our Nation's cybersecurity posture.

12. Cyber Security Risk Management Practices are Insufficient—A lack of agreed upon cybersecurity risk management practices, frameworks, tools, methods, etc. is leading to confusion. Cyber security risk management science is in its infancy, but hacker techniques are sophisticated.

13. There is a National Shortage of Security Experts. Most organizations do not have an expert who understands the emerging security threats, threat actors, vulnerabilities, and the like as it takes time and expertise and cannot simply be assigned to existing staff. The large companies and government agencies are "buying" their experts, leaving most of U.S. companies with insufficient expertise. Government, private and public sectors are all facing an enormous shortage in cybersecurity talent. The subject of cybersecurity is showing up in classrooms all over the Nation to fill a worldwide shortage of 1 million openings. Symantec is the world's largest security software vendor recently reported that the demand for the cybersecurity workforce is expected to rise by 6 million professionals globally by 2019, with a projected shortfall of 1.5 million. That will leave companies and information less protected than they should be against hackers. While technology is vital to preventing, detecting and responding to security attacks, equally important are the people who determine security strategy, devise and operationalize security programs, and skillfully deploy the technologies that wall-off our critical infrastructures and information. According to CIO Magazine, cybersecurity professionals report an average salary of $116,000 which is nearly three times the national median income for full-time wage and salary workers, according to the Bureau of Labor Statistics. We need to expand our cybersecurity workforce.

Recommendations

1. Think through the Global Nature of the Issue—An international group should study the cybersecurity issues and draft a series of issues and recommendations which could feed our National Strategy. The Internet is not a U.S. thing. It is a global infrastructure with global reach and implications.

2. Develop a National Cyber Security Strategy—The Federal Government should work with government, academia, corporate America and the small business community to devise a comprehensive, bilaterally supported national security strategy that includes goals, objectives and funding sources. Establishing a front line of defense against today's immediate threats and to defend again a full spectrum of future threats is so massive that only the Federal Government could take this on. Improved awareness needs to be at the center of this strategy.

3. Focus on Power and Telecommunications—while there are many more "critical infrastructures" which need protection, all infrastructures depend upon Power and Telecommunications. Melissa Hathaway mentioned at Harvard's 2015 class entitled, Cybersecurity—The Intersection of Policy and Technology that these two infrastructures should be the first order of priority protection in the United States and around the world. Funding the improved security of 20 infrastructures has proven impossible, so a strategy to focus resources on power and telecommunications seems reasonable.

4. Pass Cybersecurity Information Sharing Act of 2015 (CISA)—Congress should pass a cybersecurity bill that encourages and incentivizes private companies to share data with the Federal Government. While the ISACs are improving information sharing, companies are still reluctant to share. A bill that would incentivize the sharing of cybersecurity threat information between the private sector and the government and among private sector entities and responds to the massive and mounting threat to national and economic security from cyber events. The bill should also look to improve the cybersecurity of both public and private computer networks by increasing awareness of both threats and countermeasures.

5. Pass Federal Data Breach Notification Law of 2015—allow for uniform definition and application of data breach policy, while providing exemptions to improve the flexibility to hone the law to meet specific needs. Consistent with the February 5, 2015 testimony of American Bankers Association Senior Vice President Doug Johnson, we support 1) pre-empting inconsistent state laws and regulations in favor of strong Federal data protection and notification standards, 2) strong national data protection and consumer notification standards with effective enforcement provisions, and 3) the costs of a data breach should ultimately be borne by the entity that incurs the breach.

6. Improve grant opportunities and funding for research in cybersecurity, with an emphasis on risk management practices and security awareness solutions. The National Science Foundation and others could be equipped with the resources to focus on these two very important areas. While cybersecurity technology-based research funding is available, these two important focus areas should be emphasized. SBIR programs can also look to write these two areas into their solicitations. Applied research should be emphasized.

7. Consider Requiring Cyber Insurance—Organizations which operate a digital capability might need to carry cyber insurance. Many businesses have been resistant to spend money in this area. Congress may consider either 1) requiring a basic level of cyber insurance for those organizations that meet a certain profile, or 2) requiring a specific set of mitigating controls that all organization should implement. Examples are already documented in the SBA Small Business Security Standard and the NIST Small Business Security Standard.

8. Build Upon Existing NSA/DHS CAE Program—This program is a tremendous success story and should be enhanced to include many other audiences (*i.e.,* industry, high schools, veterans, etc.). Scholarships and financial support must be made available to make the cybersecurity field an attractive career choice to close the gap on the million job shortage we are facing. The CAE program is a huge success and the credit goes to the thought leaders in the Federal Government that anticipated the cybersecurity issue and the resource shortage it would create. We advise the President to consider expanding this program with funding, so that more educational, research, and outreach capacity is created to serve the needs of government and industry (companies small and large). We advise the expansion of the Scholarship for Service Program (SFS) at NSA, DoD, and NSF, including expanding the number of scholarships and the places scholarship students can pay back their scholarship. For example, can we make it possible for a SFS student to complete his/her service at a critical infrastructure owned and operated by the private sector such as a power supplier or an Internet Service Provider?

9. Devise More Effective (and Affordable) Cyber Security Training and Educational Programs—Citizens and businesses alike must be trained in to run technology securely in this digital age. Making cybersecurity training and education available and affordable is the key. One such example is the Program in Bank Technology Management that Kirby Davidson at the Graduate School of Banking at the University of Wisconsin has developed. This Program launched in April, 2011 and was capped at 50 students (which filled in two weeks). The Program is a blend of technology and security honed specifically to the community banking audience. The program includes 12 hours of "ethical hacking", where students download and execute common hacking tools so they understand what tools the adversary has in the arsenal. After the training is completed, they have a better understanding of the adversary and more importantly can return to their businesses and help secure our infrastructure.

Conclusion

Electronic products and delivery systems are the future in banking and beyond, and if businesses cannot understand and resource their technology and security requirements then they will likely be left behind. We agree with the White House's conclusion in their recent cybersecurity legislative proposal that, at least with respect to cyber terrorists, the vulnerability of the electricity grid poses one of the most severe exposures to our country's critical infrastructure. The fact that a computer Programmer or hacker in another country could cause the partial or complete disruption of this Nation's grid is, to say the least, extremely disturbing, but is beyond the scope and expertise of businesses to respond. However, small and medium-sized financial institutions need representation at the table, and we encourage the President to consider including this voice as small and medium-sized financial institutions and businesses are the majority, not the minority, of America n businesses.

We conclude with this thought. In 2009, President Obama stated:

> *We count on computer networks to **deliver** our oil **and gas**, our power and our water. We rely on them for public transportation **and air traffic** control... But just as we failed in the past to invest in our physical infrastructure – our roads, our bridges and rails – **we've failed** to invest in the security of our digital infrastructure... This status quo is **no longer acceptable** -not when there's so much at stake. We **can and** we must do better.*
> Source: President Obama, May 29, 2009

The first question is, "have we made enough progress over the past six years"? No doubt we are improved, but so have the capabilities of our cyber adversaries. With the explosion of the Internet, digital currencies, and the next generation of networked technologies, organizations will become more dependent upon technology to grow their businesses and reach more customers. The second question is, "are we prepared for the future"? Customers will interact with technology even more frequently and intimately than today, and cyber criminals will be more savvy and well-funded than ever before. The risk to our Nation is clear that a cyber-terrorist thousands of miles away can hold a citizen, organization or country hostage with binary attacks. When this happens, it is not simply Microsoft or Oracle who must respond. We need a strategy that focuses resources, builds capabilities in the areas we need, informs consumers and business leaders of their responsibilities, promote information sharing and customer notification, and builds the cyber workforce of tomorrow.

Chairman Thune, Ranking Member Nelson and Members of the Senate Committee on Commerce, Science, and Transportation, thank you for the opportunity to participate in this important and timely hearing. Dakota State University looks forward to working with all stakeholders to operationalize the President's vision of a safe electronic infrastructure for all businesses to use. We applaud the President in making cybersecurity an Administration priority, and concur with the President's comments that the "cyber threat is one of the most serious economic and national security challenges we face as a nation." To make an impact, policy must change, resource allocation must change, and a more comprehensive approach must be deployed.

We want to thank you again for your leadership and this opportunity to appear before you.

APPENDIX A

Growth of the Internet

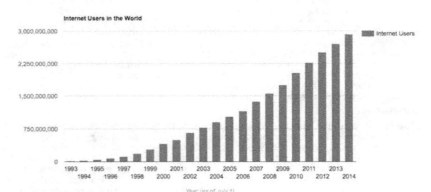

Rank*	Country	Internet Users	1 Year Growth %	1 Year User Growth	Total Country Population	1 Yr Population Change (%)	Penetration (% of Pop. with Internet)	Country's share of World Population	Country's share of World Internet Users
1	China	641,601,070	4%	24,021,070	1,393,783,836	0.59%	46.03%	19.24%	21.97%
2	United States	279,834,232	7%	17,754,869	322,583,006	0.79%	86.75%	4.45%	9.58%
3	India	243,198,922	14%	29,859,598	1,267,401,849	1.22%	19.19%	17.50%	8.33%
4	Japan	109,252,912	8%	7,668,535	126,999,808	-0.11%	86.03%	1.75%	3.74%
5	Brazil	107,822,831	7%	6,884,333	202,033,670	0.83%	53.37%	2.79%	3.69%
6	Russia	84,437,793	10%	7,494,536	142,467,651	-0.26%	59.27%	1.97%	2.89%
7	Germany	71,727,551	2%	1,525,829	82,652,256	-0.09%	86.78%	1.14%	2.46%
8	Nigeria	67,101,452	16%	9,365,590	178,516,904	2.82%	37.59%	2.46%	2.30%
9	United Kingdom	57,075,826	3%	1,574,653	63,489,234	0.56%	89.90%	0.88%	1.95%
10	France	55,429,382	3%	1,521,369	64,641,279	0.54%	85.75%	0.89%	1.90%

47

Growth of Internet of Things

How big is the Internet of Things?

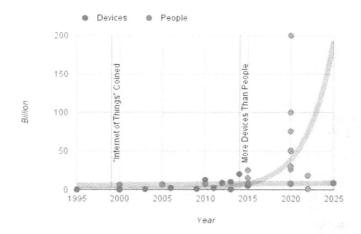

Source: Author's calculations based on data from ABI Research (2013), Business Insider
(2013), Cisco (2013, 2015), EMC (2014), Ericsson (2011), Forbes (2013), Gartner (2013),
Hammersmith Group (2010), Intel (2014), Internet Census (2012), Internet World Stats
(multiple), Machina Research (2013), Navigant Research (2013).

The CHAIRMAN. Thank you, Dr. Streff.

We will turn now to our final witness, and that is Dr. Josh Pauli.

STATEMENT OF JOSHUA J. PAULI, PH.D., PROFESSOR OF CYBER SECURITY, DAKOTA STATE UNIVERSITY

Dr. PAULI. Thank you. So I live a mile from campus, so I get to go last.

[Laughter.]

Dr. PAULI. It would be easy for me to say I have nothing more to add, but, of course, anybody who knows me knows that is not true.

So we have heard a lot of bad news, we have heard a lot of doom and gloom. I have some good news. I have some excellent news.

Everything you have heard up here is true, right? Breaches, shortages of people, more complex attacks—100 percent true. But what we are dealing with mostly is a people shortage. So the good news is we have everything in place to fix this. We don't need to reinvent anything; we just need to use what we have.

For those of you that were here this morning and met with our students and saw some of the research projects from our CyberCorps students, I think you would know that, and you would agree with me, right? We have a people problem. We don't have a shiny red box thing or a new tool thing, right? We have a people shortage.

So my idea—and I don't have a script, right? I have notes. So that is just kind of how I go. You have my written testimony. I am more than happy to go line by line with you if you would like, but I would like everybody——

The CHAIRMAN. That won't be necessary.

Dr. PAULI. What?

The CHAIRMAN. That won't be necessary.

[Laughter.]

Dr. PAULI. That won't be necessary, yes. You have seen my work before.

[Laughter.]

The CHAIRMAN. No.

Dr. PAULI. So think of a funnel; everybody think of a funnel. And what we need to pop out of the end of the funnel is a higher quantity and a higher quality of graduate. We don't need anything else, right? We have everything else.

You heard our students this morning talk about let's get back to the basics—strong passwords, segmented networks, some of those fundamental things that, if we had this hearing 10 years ago or 20 year ago we are still talking about.

So let's consider this funnel that we need to have a higher number and a higher quality of person pop out of the end. So what we need to do is we need to make this funnel wider. And to do that, we need to reach down lower into our middle schools and our high schools to excite and retain and recruit students into cybersecurity.

Some of you are familiar with the GenCyber summer camp, Generation Cyber, which is a joint project from the National Security Agency and the National Science Foundation. Touched 1,500 students this year.

The crazy thing is there was no dedicated funding to that project, right? There were kind of these leftovers from NSA, some leftovers from NSF that they were able to scrape together and fund camps for 1,500 students. Right? Fifty percent which were females. That is a lot better than the 18 percent of females that enter computer-science-related fields. We had two slam-dunk camps here on campus, right? One for girls, 100 girls, 200 co-ed. Right?

So we need to expand GenCyber. So if it is NSF, great, let's do that. If it is NSA, great, let's do that. If it is somebody else that wants to help, let's do that. But we don't need to reinvent the wheel.

Second, we need to continue to develop our university programs and our faculty. You see this through the Center of Academic Excellence designations the senator mentioned. DSU is 1 of 14 cyber operations schools. We were one of the first four in 2012, right? That is a very, very elite club, right?

So it is great to say DSU is right there with MIT and Carnegie Mellon and Northeastern, right? That is fun, and our students bear the benefit of that. Those types of programs that are upping the ante for our academic programs are needed to continue.

We also need to fund our university students through programs like the CyberCorps program. I don't know one university, one student who is in a CyberCorps award, or one government entity who takes these students on that doesn't think this is a fantastic program. Think about that. Government loves it, academics love it, and students love it? I don't know of another program in existence that has that triad.

CyberCorps is $45 million a year, which you think, like, wow, that is really good. The entire National Science Foundation is $7.7 billion. So CyberCorps is barely one-half of 1 percent of the entire foundation. We need to increase that. Everybody knows and everybody agrees that CyberCorps is important. We need to increase that.

For example, DSU has one of the largest CyberCorps programs. We give out 10 new scholarships a year. I can look anybody in the eye and tell you we could fund 30 per year of students who deserve that program, who deserve that scholarship. And I think that story is the same across the nation.

So, once we fund them, we need to find them jobs, right? So we have some efforts going, which you have heard, right? NIST is all over this with their Cybersecurity Framework, which businesses of all sizes should be implementing, right? We need to continue to figure out ways to get that into the hands of everybody.

We need to continue to look at the NICE framework, the NICE job framework that says, if you have these types of skills and abilities, these types of jobs would be good for you. We need to implement that framework not only through government but across everywhere, right? SDN should be able to post a job that said, "Here are your NICE framework details," and a student could say, "Wow, that kind of matches my profile. I should apply to that." That framework is out there; we need to use it.

And I think what we are seeing is more industries becoming more aware of cyber, right? So right here in little Madison, South Dakota, we have two power entities that are all over cyber, right?

So some of you may have heard East River here in town hired some new CIO, right? Some wacky college professor left DSU, right? That is a huge testament to East River's forward thinking on cybersecurity. We need more of that. We need to help with that.

And then their friends—I think they are friends. I think Heartland and East River get along, right? Heartland, led by Russ Olson, not only taking care of his own house but partnered with Helix Security, a security firm here in town, to look out for their customers, right? So how crazy is that? A power company pushing down cyber guidance to their customers. That is pretty awesome, and we need to continue to grow some of that stuff.

So, in closing, if you think of my funnel, we need to widen the funnel, we need to dump more kids into the top when they are 10 and 12 years old so that when they are 23 they pop out and they are ready.

Thank you.

[The prepared statement of Dr. Pauli follows:]

PREPARED STATEMENT OF JOSHUA J. PAULI, PH.D., PROFESSOR OF CYBER SECURITY, DAKOTA STATE UNIVERSITY

Recent DSU Successes

There is much to celebrate at Dakota State University in Madison, SD as our cybersecurity programs are experiencing explosive growth in both the quantity and quality of student enrollments. Since 2012, our three undergraduate degrees most closely aligned with cybersecurity, those being Cyber Operations, Network Security, and Computer Science, have seen an 83 percent increase in students from 382 in the fall of 2012 to 698 in the fall of 2015 as introduced in the table below.

	2012 Fall	2013 Fall	2014 Fall	2015 Fall
Cyber Operations, Network Security, & Computer Science BS Degrees at DSU	382	470	569	698

Approximately 400 of these students are on-campus and account for an estimated 1/3 of the entire on-campus student population of DSU, while the remaining 300 are online students from around the country. Our graduate programs, which include a Masters in Applied Computer Science, a Masters in Information Assurance, and a Doctorate in Cyber Security are also growing rapidly as Dakota State University's reputation for high-quality education in cybersecurity at a reasonable price continues to expand across the country.

Much of this student growth at DSU can be traced back to three main milestones. First, DSU was awarded a grant from the National Science Foundation (NSF) in 2011 to join the CyberCorps SFS program to award full ride scholarships and stipends to high-achieving students that are interested in working for the government in a cybersecurity position after graduation. 44 DSU students have been awarded this scholarship and we've placed 100 percent of our interns and graduates in government positions around the country.

Second, DSU's Cyber Operations undergraduate degree program was designated as a Center of Academic Excellence in Cyber Operations (CAE–CO) by the National Security Agency (NSA) as one of the first four such Centers in 2012. This is a very exclusive honor for DSU as there are currently only 14 designated programs in the Nation. Less than 25 percent of university applying to the CAE–CO program meet the stringent requirements for this designation and DSU is widely viewed as one of top Cyber Operations programs in the Nation by the government and academic communities alike for our deeply technical focus and hands-on approach.

Third, DSU entered an academic articulation agreement with the NSA in 2015 to award DSU academic credit towards our Cyber Operations undergraduate program for education and training that NSA employees, primarily military personnel, complete as part of their work at the Agency. This articulation agreement is the first such agreement in the history of the NSA and will enable these employees to be retained by the NSA or Department of Defense (DoD) after graduating from DSU. This is also likely the first such agreement by any Federal Government agen-

51

cy dedicated to cybersecurity education, which has huge potential for all agencies to help attract and retain top cybersecurity graduates.

Current Threat

Despite the good news at DSU and the focus of many academic, government, and professional organizations on cybersecurity threats today, I believe the United States would lose a cyber conflict between nation states if it took place today. My worries go beyond the data breaches that have dominated the headlines in recent months, but instead extend into the military, intelligence, and business competitiveness arenas of our country. We have an extreme shortage of qualified professionals in the cybersecurity domain across both public and private sectors. We must greatly expand the quantity and quality of the cyber workforce to ensure the necessary knowledge, skills, and abilities are in place to help protect the Nation and conduct cyber operations. We can help solve this capacity problem with existing programs that have already proven to be highly effective and successful as partially discussed in my testimony of S. 1353: Cybersecurity Enhancement Act of 2014.

The Way Ahead

To meet the cybersecurity personnel needs in public and private sectors, we must increase the numbers in every stage of the process in order to end up with a tangible increase in the number of qualified professional. The funnel introduced below is an accurate representation of the processes that must occur when trying to grow the cyber workforce.

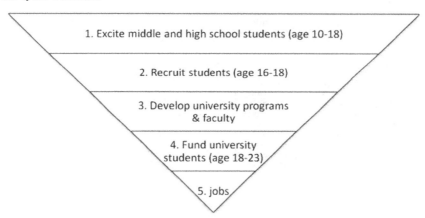

1. Excite Middle and High School Students (Age 10–18)

We must increase the funding to the GenCyber Summer Camp program that has been offering cybersecurity summer camps to middle school students, high school students, and K–12 teachers since 2014 on university campuses around the Nation. GenCyber is a joint effort by NSF and NSA that administered 43 camps at 29 universities in 18 different states during the summer of 2015 that supported approximately 1,500 students and 300 teachers. The student population was 50 percent female, which is a dramatic increase from the 18 percent of females that enter computer science programs at the university level. GenCyber has been a tremendous success despite never having dedicated funding from the NSA or NSF in the last two years. It has only been funded by "left over" funding. In order to expand GenCyber, and other similar programs with the goal of increasing student interest at a young age, dedicated funding and programs need to be established. Expansion of this program should also include year-round programming for interested students by the way of after-school programs, college-level courses, and other engagements integrated into the academic year of middle school and high school students. This education of young minds is critical in order to increase the quantity of students that at least consider going into a cybersecurity field of study at the university level. Programs like GenCyber are the entry point to the funnel, thus it needs to pull from a very wide audience of students and teachers.

52

2. Recruit Students (Age 16–18)

Direct recruitment of high school students to university programs is not a formal aspect of GenCyber as the camps are 100 percent about cybersecurity education and to excite students to pursue cybersecurity educational and professional pathways. Any recruitment is secondary to the goal of the camps and only happens organically. We need to develop a formal recruitment plan for students that is overt in its mission and can be scaled nationwide. I believe this is an excellent project for NIST's Security Outreach and Integration (SOI) Group and the National Initiative for Cybersecurity Education (NICE) to work alongside universities and government agencies to develop a "full court press" approach to recruiting students directly into cybersecurity academic programs and career pathways. With the support of NIST, NSF, GenCyber, and universities around the nation, a recruitment plan to target this population would further widen the audience of upcoming cybersecurity professionals.

3. Develop University Programs and Faculty

Our university programs must continue to grow and evolve in order to keep up with the demands of the professional workplace and the incoming students. While there are capacity building funds attached to various grant programs, the current level of support must be increased to support more academic programs in additional ways. NIST's National Initiative for Cybersecurity Education (NICE) is an ideal mechanism to provide additional resources into the ongoing development of our programs and faculty around the Nation. The NICE Workforce Framework is a tremendous effort to identify and classify the necessary knowledge, skills, and abilities (KSAs) that are required in today's cybersecurity workforce. Now is the time to take this same framework and provide assistance to educational institutions to ensure our programs and faculty are positioned to implement the framework.

An existing mechanism within the Department of Defense (DoD) that needs to be mimicked across the Nation is University affiliated Research Centers (UARCs) that enable a closer working relationship among government agencies, university faculty members, and university students. UARCs are very similar to Federally Funded Research and Development Centers (FFRDCs) in that an external entity, such as a university or non-profit corporation, conducts research and development for the U.S. Government. It's now time to have such Centers dedicated to solving the problem of attracting and educating the next generation of cybersecurity professionals. These Centers would be the hub of activity for government agencies, universities, and high schools across the Nation to support the mission of increasing the quantity and quality of cybersecurity professionals.

Currently the only Department of Commerce FFRDC is the National Cybersecurity Center of Excellence (NCCoE) that is dedicated to cybersecurity best practices across critical infrastructures, but multiple Departments of the U.S. Government can sponsor an FFRDC, so the Center can conduct research for both Departments. There are many moving parts to such an endeavor, but we must better identify and coordinate our efforts to cybersecurity recruitment and education and UARCs and FFRDCs are a great approach to this coordination.

4. Fund University Students (Age 18–23)

NSF is the source for 89 percent of all Federal funding to computer science and cybersecurity at our universities, so we look to the NSF as almost the sole source of Federal funding to our programs. The NSF's CyberCorps SFS program is widely viewed by government and academia alike as the most effective way to place top students in cybersecurity careers within the government. The program has achieved the rare feat of gaining positive endorsements from government agencies, university faculty members, and scholarship students alike. CyberCorps SFS has supported 1,750 students since the programs inception in 2002 and approximately 200 new students per year, which is a drop in the bucket compared to the need we face. The NSF's Graduate Research Fellow (GRF) program, which spans all academic disciplines and is the NSF program CyberCorps is most commonly referenced with, supports 2,000 students per year. The CyberCorps budget for 2015 is $45M, which is 0.62 percent of the NSF's $7.7B 2015 appropriation and just 13.5 percent of GRF's 2015 appropriation. An increase to the CyberCorps program is a wise investment for the future of cybersecurity professionals within government agencies.

5. Place Students in Internships and Graduates in Careers

Any efforts to continue to streamline the hiring process of student into internships and graduates into careers is greatly appreciated by everyone involved. Continued work on raising salaries for the most critical cybersecurity positions in all government agencies is also a positive step forward and should continue. It's unrealistic to expect government jobs to keep pace with private sector pay, but it must at least be close enough for the student to consider accepting the government position. Often times the application and hiring process is by far the worst experience for students and graduates. These delays also result in government agencies missing out on students and graduates that actually want to work for them, but get hung up during the hiring process. This is a topic that has received discussion for several years between academia and government, but should continue to be researched for a way to make the process better on an on-going basis.

We must also find better ways to get students who are not CyberCorps scholars placed at government agencies. As an example, DSU has 10 new CyberCorps students per year, but realistically has 20–25 students that deserve the scholarship and another 20–25 students per year that would make perfectly capable hires into government cybersecurity positions. But because the process is so convoluted and slow, these 50 non-CyberCorps students can not get noticed by government agencies and are forced to take jobs, often times lesser jobs, outside of government. There are countless students around the Nation who would gladly work for the government, but they are so turned off by the hiring process that they don't even consider public service.

Conclusion

The demand for cybersecurity professional is only going to increase in both public and private sectors. We need to act now to help fill this demand with the types of graduates that are well prepared for the workplace of the coming years. Although there is much work to be done to generate the quantity and quality of the cyber workforce, there is a proven plan to achieve noticeable progress towards this goal. Now we need to execute this plan.

The CHAIRMAN. Well, thank you, Dr. Pauli.

And thank all of you for terrific testimony and great insights, all of which I think will be very useful as we continue to examine these issues and look for solutions, at least to the degree that solutions are going to be found in Washington, D.C., and Congress. And there are some things that we do need to do, we realize, and some things that we really need to stay out of the way.

But I want to come back to this workforce issue since we are here on the campus of Dakota State University. And, Dr. Pauli, I will start with you, since you kind of wrapped up with that.

You mentioned in your written remarks that there are 10 new CyberCorps students per year but, realistically, that DSU has 20 to 25 students that deserve the scholarship, another 25 students per year that would make perfectly capable hires into government cybersecurity positions.

And then you also indicated that there are many students who are turned off by the Government hiring process. So I am wondering maybe if you could elaborate on the current hiring issues that your students encounter.

And then I would like to, after you conclude, just for those of you on the panel who employ people—and we have a couple of folks in government, some private sector—as you are looking for people to hire in your operations, what you are looking for, and how might DSU best prepare students for those types of opportunities.

Dr. PAULI. Yes. So you are absolutely right. I am happy you read my written testimony. So you are right. We give out 10 of these scholarships per year. We do have 20 to 25 who absolutely deserve it.

And then we have this other group that, even without the CyberCorps scholarship, are ready, willing, and able to work for the government. And part of it is because of our geographical location, right? We don't have Google in our backyard saying, "Give me all of your best students." We have some in the region, but we have 700 cybersecurity students at DSU.

So, yes, we have capacity. We have better students now than we ever have, and that is going to keep getting better.

In terms of hiring, getting hired into the government, it is a very disheartening thing when the first thing a student hears, right, they go out to a website—NSA, CIA, NIST, doesn't matter—and the first thing that they are told is, "Go out to USAJOBS.gov and apply." So, being studious, they go out and do that. And they wait, and they wait, and they wait. There is no acknowledgment that their application was received. There is no, "Here is the timeline of your application and where it is in the process." And then, months later, they may or may not get notified, right?

So I think too many of our students—the CyberCorps students are locked in. I make those students go through that process. They have to do it. But we are losing a big chunk of students who could and want to go do that work during that slow process. And it is easy to bash HR. I am not bashing HR. I am bashing the hiring process.

So a student who is not on CyberCorps wants to go work at NSA, they apply, they don't hear anything for 6 months. Well, in the meantime, it is really easy for them to say, I'm 23 years old, I have the world by the tail, I want to go out and do great things, but I haven't heard anything, and I need a job, so I will take a job that is a rung or two down.

And we are missing the boat there with that population.

The CHAIRMAN. Yes.

Anybody else want to talk about, in terms of hiring, when you are looking for people to work in this particular space, notwithstanding the Federal hiring issues? And I don't know if you can speak to that, you know, either NIST or NSF.

And then, any of the guys that are working in the private world, any observations that you might have about how best to get our young people ready and expedite that hiring process so we can address the deficit, which Dr. Streff pointed out, which is a million positions relative to the number of people that are available to fill them.

Mr. PULSE. I will jump in here, if you don't mind.

Great stuff, Josh.

One thing I will say is I think that private industry needs to get over one thing, and that is, if you are out looking for, you know, a new hire and they don't happen to particularly have an industry-level skill set, whether it is in the financial sector, healthcare sector, insurance, or whatever it is, organizations tend to shy away from them. This person doesn't know banking," "This person doesn't know health care," or whatever. But, from my perspective, and hopefully some agree here, this security thing is agnostic, it is industry-agnostic.

I mean, we talked about, you know, binary obfuscation this morning. Bits and bytes are bits and bytes, right, whether you are in a bank or a hospital or the Federal Government. And securing against, you know, APTs and everything that is out there, I think, culturally, now, a lot of—and, again, I am big on this culture thing—a lot of it has to do with that. And I think we just need to get over the hump of, you know, the old industry thing.

The CHAIRMAN. Being industry-specific.

Mr. PULSE. Exactly.

The CHAIRMAN. OK. All right. Thank you.

Mr. STINE. Yes, I think that is a very important point.

I think one of the other realizations here is that the technical skills are very important, the traditional computer science and the engineering courses are absolutely critical, but cybersecurity is a very multidisciplinary area. So there is a need for not only those kind of bits-and-bytes technical skills but also looking beyond to some of the psychologies and the sociologies, some of the softer sciences, the finances.

Because there is very much a human-centric element to all of cybersecurity, as well, not only in terms of working with kind of the end user, so to speak, but also developing solutions that are going to be understandable and usable and effective for those end users and those organizations that have missions and business objectives to accomplish.

The CHAIRMAN. Anybody else?

Mark, go ahead.

Mr. SHLANTA. I just wanted to add I am probably someone who benefits from the slow process of the Federal Government hiring, you know, in that——

[Laughter.]

Dr. PAULI. I wasn't going to say that, Mark. I wasn't going to say it.

[Laughter.]

Mr. SHLANTA.—that, you know, just right up the road, less than an hour from where SDN is located, we have this school. And we have a number of graduates of Dakota State on our staff.

But I think other things that businesses can do to help develop staff—we have a long history of internships, and I would encourage all in the private sector to work with the educational facilities, put the students to work over the summer. No matter where they go and where they come from, they will bring skills to you, and they will probably learn something, I know they will learn something from you and take it other places. But all of that, just think of that at a level of information-sharing, as well, in terms of just developing the talent.

But I think one of the things we have to do as businesses, as well, is, in addition to the internships that I talked about, like, we worked with Josh and Dr. Streff in DSU with that cyber camp this summer. When it filled so quickly, they ran out of budget; we helped them with expanding that platform. And it really is South Dakota's workforce that I was most interested in at that point, in terms of developing it, and businesses can step in and assist.

And then, really, the last thing that I would add is really just that, you know, the continued prioritization, kind of what Eric was talking about, you know, that cyber professionals can add, really, to just about any business. They don't have to be a technology business like ours. And businesses across the country need to recognize that. And that will grow the workforce.

The CHAIRMAN. Good.

Anything else?

Go ahead.

Mr. EPSTEIN. Just a brief comment, that we agree at NSF that we need to widen the funnel, as you say, and bring in more students. SFS can't do it all, of course, but we agree.

There has been an average of about 170 students a year for the past few years nationwide graduating from SFS. And Dakota State is the 15th biggest in terms of number of students nationwide, which is a pretty good number for a small school. As a percentage basis, I would guess that you are probably the highest in the country, and that is great. And we do need to expand it as funding allows.

Dr. STREFF. And if I could make a couple comments.

The first is there is a huge multiplying effect with these scholarship programs. It is not about 10 kids, right? Josh can talk about the numbers. We had 100 kids before the program, and then we get the program and it is 700. There is a huge multiplying factor here that happens.

The second thing that I would ask for NSF and others on the Committee to think about is the scholarship needs to be paid back at a government agency. I would ask that we look at that. How about a power company, or how about at a telco? I mean, if we are prioritizing infrastructures high, like power and telecommunications, and they need help, isn't that the point, getting our best and brightest there? Can they pay back their service there?

And I know that that is not a part of the deal right now, but I would ask for us to look at those critical infrastructures and say, how do we help?

The CHAIRMAN. OK.

If there are any students who want to ask any of these guys a question about any of these workforce issues, think about that for a minute, and we will come back to this before we kind of exhaust this subject. Because I think this is an important one and very relevant to the broader discussion about cybersecurity.

I want to shift gears for just a minute and go back to something that, Mark, you talked about in your remarks, and that is, you know, you pointed out that these cyber attacks don't confine themselves to populated areas or big businesses. This hits rural areas, South Dakota, and the examples you put up about the state of South Dakota and Sioux Falls governments.

And then you mentioned in your testimony that 95 percent of these cyber incidents, security incidents, involve human error and that "businesses should therefore"—and I am quoting from your written testimony—"improve the cyber literacy of their workforce and limit their employees' access and ability to distribute sensitive information."

So you have touched on this in your testimony. I wondered if you could elaborate on what SDN is doing to promote increased cyber literacy. And maybe if anybody else wants to jump in on that, too. What are we doing to educate better the people that we are involved with—employees, clients, et cetera—when it comes to just literacy about cyber issues and the threats?

Mr. SHLANTA. I will address a few of the items that we are doing at SDN. And, when you start to think about them, they are really basic things, but apparently not enough companies are doing it.

A variety of testimony today talked about the levels of attacks with vulnerabilities where patches existed for over a year, as an example. So, frankly, patches, the security patches, applying them on a timely basis. We have a daily update into our patch program, and, frankly, if there is a zero-day threat that is identified, there could be multiple updates during the day. And that is just one way to handle those types of things.

Password control. Strong passwords, meaningful passwords, passwords that have to be changed, passwords that can't be repeated. Those are as simple as locking the front door. If you think of your network as your house and your password is the way into the house, change the locks from time to time, you know? It is the way to keep the bad guys out.

Solid network administration. We have 180 employees at SDN, and 180 employees don't need to touch every file on the network, as an example. So making sure you are limiting access to your staff. That way, if there is a compromise and someone's credentials are compromised and a bad guy gets in, they can only go as far as that person is authorized to get into the network.

And, even remote access—you talked about Office of Personnel Management, two-step authentication. That is really one of the easiest things, in addition to solid password control and network administration.

So those are a couple of things that we do and really every business could do, but they take education, they take discipline. They are just good, solid business practices.

The CHAIRMAN. OK.

Anybody else?

Mr. EPSTEIN. I think you hit on a really important point, which is that cybersecurity isn't just a technical issue; it is a human issue, as well, as Kevin mentioned a few minutes ago.

We set up a new activity within the SaTC program at NSF that I lead to bring together social scientists and computer scientists to explore some of these questions. For example, why don't users install patches when they get warnings, when they get messages?

How many of you have gotten that message, would you like to install an upgrade, and you say, no, no, no, I am busy, I am busy, I am too busy on Facebook, I don't want to install the update now? We all do this. I did it on my phone yesterday, or today. We have to understand this better.

We have to understand why users pick poor passwords and how we can encourage them to do a better job, other than beating them up all the time, because we know beating them up doesn't really work very effectively. It has negative side effects. They may choose a good password today and then use it on 10 different websites because they can't remember 10 good passwords.

Are there differences between different groups? We have a project we are funding to talk to teenagers and college students in different ethnic groups. Do Hispanic kids, African-American kids, white kids, Native American kids, do they have different attitudes toward privacy that lead them to make different decisions about

how they treat data online and how they behave online? Do teenagers behave differently from senior citizens? What motivates senior citizens to behave differently?

We have to understand the people aspect, not just the technology
aspect, because as we understand the people aspect, then we will
be able to come up with better solutions that will work for the Nation as a whole and not just for a subset.

The CHAIRMAN. Good.

Anybody else on this?

Mr. PULSE. If I can add, again, for me, it kind of comes back to
this security culture thing. And, you know, obviously, Mark is at
the top of his organization, and they take security very seriously
there.

You know, organizations are spending millions and millions of
dollars, or they can spend millions of dollars on a hardware/soft-
ware secure infrastructure, but if there is not a secure culture,
right, if, you know, an employee is going to click on that, you know,
phishing link or whatever it is, I mean, they effectively become the
prettiest horse in the glue factory, right? They spent all that money
for what? And, to me, it starts at the top.

I mean, I commend Dakota State University. I just learned this
today at lunch. Every student at this university has to take a computer course, has to understand computing and, as an extension,
security. I mean, I think, you know, all STEM education should
really add a security component to it, because, again, culturally,
you know, as we go down the road, it is going to become more important, more and more important.

The CHAIRMAN. We had a meeting a few weeks ago in Sioux
Falls, very well attended, and it was a STOP.THINK.CONNECT.
event that was sponsored by the National Cybersecurity Alliance.
And it was, you know, designed to recognize how important it is
to increase our cyber awareness. And one of the things that came
out of that in the discussion was that the two most commonly used
passwords are "123456" and "password."

[Laughter.]

The CHAIRMAN. So, strong passwords. They talked a lot about
two-step authentication, not opening up the phishing links, thing
like that that we can do that are fairly straightforward, simple
fixes that are precautions that every individual ought to be taking
when it comes to our own cybersecurity.

Just out of curiosity, and this is more of kind of a general question, but you all work in this field, so what is the thing, the biggest
threat, the biggest vulnerability that you see as you sort of look out
on the horizon, the thing that might, as people who are concerned
about cybersecurity, keep you up at night as we look down the
road?

And a couple of you commented, which I thought this was a good
observation—and maybe, Eric, you mentioned this—that oftentimes
you come up with a prescription or a remedy and it fixes something
for a time, but too often, you know, then the bad guys figure out
a way around it and come up with a different solution. And you
have to constantly be upgrading and looking for new safeguards
and new firewalls and new ways to protect not only critical infrastructure but even people's personal information.

So, you know, given the fact that there is a constant evolving threat matrix out there, as you kind of look at this issue in the bigger 30,000 foot context, what is it that worries you the most?

Yes, sir. Mr. Epstein.

Mr. EPSTEIN. Senator, what worries me the most is the lifetime of our systems. As we go to Internet of Things systems, the average lifetime is going to go from 2 years with a phone or 3 years with a laptop to 10, 15, 20 years. I don't know how to design a computer system today that is still going to be secure 20 years from now.

And as an example of this, my research is in voting system security. And I have talked to some of you about this over lunch. Systems that we approve for voting today are still going to be in use 10 or 20 years from now. How do I design a system that protects our democracy that is going to be secure against a threat that I can't even conceive of?

So that is what keeps me up, is worrying about how I can come up with anything today that is going to be able to evolve and continue to be protected.

In the Katrina disaster, the water system in New Orleans shut down and they had to restart it. It was the first time in over 100 years that they had restarted the water system in New Orleans, and they had to figure—there was obviously no one around who was there when they started it the last time.

Do we have people who will know how to fix the problems with our Internet of Things technologies when they start breaking down 10 or 20 years from now, which is several lifetimes in terms of technology?

The CHAIRMAN. Should the threats that come from a nation-state or just, you know, a criminal hacker or a hacktivist be treated or judged any differently? I mean, obviously, some that are coming from a nation-state are threats to our critical infrastructure and should be taken very, very seriously. But how do you discriminate between those types of threats?

And when we are trying to stop something, we are trying to stop everything, and does the same level of commitment have to be there for the criminal hacker as there is for some of the more, I guess, serious threats to our—as you described, I think, threats to our democracy?

Mr. EPSTEIN. I think we have to address it for all of the attackers, because what today's nation-state can do tomorrow's teenage hacker in their basement can do. The sort of attacks we see today that some of these other witnesses have talked about, when I went to college, were unimaginable. We had things we did, but they were a whole lot simpler.

The things that we are seeing now, what we are seeing as today's nation-states' attacks, in 10 years, in 20 years, will be everywhere. And so we have to come up with the defenses and learn to deal with every class of attacker, because it is going to be everybody. Everybody is going to be the same.

The CHAIRMAN. Anybody else, what keeps you up at night?

Yes, go ahead.

Mr. STINE. I was going to add on to Mr. Epstein's point. There are many threat actors, threat adversaries out there. I think the one constant that we see is really focusing on the impact. So, regardless of whether it is a nation-state or a recreational hacker, for example, what is the impact to my organization or to me as an individual, and then being able to make informed decisions based on the potential worst-case impact of a potential attack or hack on my systems.

The CHAIRMAN. Anybody else?

Dr. STREFF. Senator, you know, I think we all talk about power-grid attacks and things like that. Those are things we have talked about already. But I am really concerned about small-business security. I am concerned that a lot of small businesses are at their tipping point anyway, and now here comes more technology and more security, and here comes a hack, and now it causes a huge disruption.

We have already seen it in the banking sector—forced consolidation, where we have gone from 12,000 banks to 7,000 banks, now we are at 6,000 charters; and health care following suit, with consolidation there, with technology and security being a part of that.

So, yes, that worries me. I mean, is Madison going to have the same number of banks or healthcare institutions, you know, 10 years from now that it does now? Things like that worry me.

The CHAIRMAN. Go ahead.

Dr. PAULI. I think across any spectrum, any industry—you know, a minute ago, we said, how can we create a system today that is going to be secure 20 years from now? We can do that. We can do that. It is not fun. It is not easy. It is not cheap. But the Department of Defense set out the Orange Book 40 years ago that talked about, these are the eight ways in which you create trustworthy software. And when they are followed, they work.

They are extremely difficult to follow, because the security of a system naturally fights against usability, performance, all these things, right? So, if you are trying to get a product to market, do you want it to be secure or do you want it to be user-friendly and fast? 99.9 percent of the time, that company is going to say, I want it to be usable, friendly, and fast. Very few systems do we get to say, no, security is the number one thing.

That is why we have breaches. That is why our software is terrible. That is why we have to keep piling on, you know, get back to the basics with all these network security measures. If we actually implemented the eight first security principles, we would be well down the road to creating robust software.

The CHAIRMAN. All right. Just—go ahead. Did you want to say something, Mark?

Mr. SHLANTA. Well, I was going to say there are two things that keep me up at night, Senator. One is my son, wondering when he is going to come home.

[Laughter.]

Mr. SHLANTA. The second is making sure that we are taking care of our customers and the data that they have entrusted to us.

One of the things that we do as a service provider—and, again, the NIST guidelines are relatively new. The CSRIC guidelines are even newer. But as we have reviewed those, they follow closely to really some of the business continuity guidelines we have followed for years.

And I think just annually or semi-annually reviewing your highest risks, your priority risks, making sure they are still current. And you just have to ask yourself the tough questions. But you don't do that as an individual. You need to bring together the operation and ask the operation what are those biggest risks and are the risks that we identified three years ago still the biggest risks or are there new ones.

So, once in a while, I ask myself that question: When was the last time we went through that process, and are we really getting to the roots of those issues?

The CHAIRMAN. Yes.

Just kind of on that, a follow-on question. But at our February hearing, when we talked about the NIST framework—and we talked a little bit about the NIST framework today—that measurement can be difficult. And even the companies that practice the best cybersecurity can fall victim to cyber incidents.

So, with that in mind, how do we measure an entity's cybersecurity posture? How do we measure success in an entity's investment in cybersecurity?

And maybe, for those of you that have had experience with it, if you could speak briefly, too, to how the NIST framework is working.

Some of the things that we worked with in the bill that we passed through the Commerce Committee and passed through the Congress and got signed into law by the president last year was maintaining a voluntary, industry-driven set of best practices that people could use. And I am just wondering, one, how that is working and, two, how do you measure the success of it. Is there a good metric? How do you quantify that?

Mr. PULSE. I will jump in here, Senator.

I mean, how do you measure if it is working? Well, ultimately, fewer breaches, right? Less lost data.

I mean, I think, from a framework perspective—and there are a lot of frameworks out there, you know, from a security perspective. You know, SANS 20 Critical Controls; the CSA has a, you know, framework, and NIST has a framework. And, I mean, I would love to see a mutual adoption of a framework that organizations can look to. And I am a fan of NIST, and I recommend NIST frameworks. I work in NIST frameworks all day every day.

And, you know, we have various organizations—Dr. Streff and I were talking earlier today, you know, that the financial institution sector came up with their own cybersecurity framework. It wasn't built on NIST's framework; it was mapped to it, but it wasn't built on it.

And, you know, why industries and that sort of thing are not adopting, you know, a similar framework is—I mean, I——

Dr. STREFF. Senator, that is a big point that Eric is bringing up there. The banking sector had a chance, as they were publishing their cybersecurity framework, to get on board with the NIST framework, which is what we were encouraging. And, instead, they came up with their own. And then they said, "Oh, here is Appendix B. It is mapped to the NIST Cybersecurity Framework."

We believe that that is a mistake, and we have been on record with them about that, the regulators. There was a comment period.

We have taken advantage of that comment period, and I know Eric's organization has, as well.

The point with frameworks is everybody has to get close to on the same framework if we are going to measure readiness. I mean, how are we doing in an industry, how are we doing as a country, how are we doing when everybody is doing security their own way.

So, at some point in time, we have to have some common elements of framework, with some flexibility for individualization, customization.

Mr. STINE. So I would add a few points.

I think there are certainly things that you can count, as has been referenced—reduced breaches, less data loss, those types of things.

I think the important point to remember in the cybersecurity framework specifically and in many risk-based approaches is that cybersecurity is a very dynamic space, and the approaches to implement cybersecurity capabilities within each organization could vary significantly from one organization to the next.

It is going to be influenced by your mission and business objectives. It is going to be influenced by your operating environment, your resourcing, your threat landscape, and ultimately the risk tolerance of your organization. Not only looking at cybersecurity but also viewing cybersecurity in the context of your mission and other dimensions of risk—financial risk, safety risk, reputational risk, for example.

I think when you look at the Cybersecurity Framework and many of the resources that NIST has produced and our standards and guidelines, they do take very much that risk management approach that you were referencing earlier, leaving the specific measurement to each individual organization because they have the context of their mission by which to view cybersecurity and understand those things that are important to their mission but also kind of be able to track the improvement.

If I could add just one more thing, in response to part of your question, the framework has been out for 18 months, roughly 18 months, version 1.0. We are very pleased with the use of the framework to date across many different industry sectors and individual companies and organizations of all shapes and sizes not only within the critical infrastructure, like the telecommunications sector, the financial sector, health care, for example, but also in non-critical infrastructure, as well.

We are seeing organizations, not only sectors as a whole for their entire membership, if you will, but also individual organizations, taking the framework, customizing it or tailoring it in a way that puts it in the context of the mission and business objectives of the organizations and the sectors.

And part of our approach at NIST is to collect those types of use cases, those experiences, those resources, and reflect those back out to the community so that others can take those, learn from those, implement them, adapt them in a meaningful way for them, and hopefully innovate on top of those for the betterment of all.

The CHAIRMAN. Thank you.

Dr. PAULI. Yes, I think it is quite simple to start, actually. If you are interested in measuring the success of the NIST framework, then let's find out who is using it.

And let's start with a captive audience. So let's start with everybody within the Department of Commerce. It came out of the Department of Commerce. How many entities within the Department of Commerce are using it? Right? Understanding that everyone will tweak it, everyone will customize it. Until we standardize things, we can't compare across and against each other.

But what we can measure and what we can measure success on is: Who is using it? Who has used it since the Enhancement Act went into effect? If you are not using it, why not? If you are using it, what do you like about it, and what stories can we share with the nonbelievers? We need to get that in order before we start comparing banks to hospitals to government agencies.

So I think we need to start with a captive audience, and I think we should start with the groups within the department.

The CHAIRMAN. Who are using it. Good.

Well, if there is anybody out here that wants to take a few minutes here, and if anybody has a question from the audience. And, again, I would open it up to students who might have questions of any of these guys on the panel here. So we will get you a microphone there. Or if you want to holler it out, holler it out.

AUDIENCE MEMBER. My name is Tanner. I am a [inaudible] student. I work at Secure Banking Solutions.

And I listened to you guys say that [inaudible]. However, I have [inaudible] things. Some of you have talked about, you know, what are we doing to make sure that access [inaudible], what are we doing to make sure that we are not going to be hacked.

As Mr. Stine said, cybersecurity is very dynamic. So what are we doing to make sure that our employees and our customers know, OK, these aren't the things that I am supposed to be doing? What are we doing to make sure that we are not being socially engineered?

Basically, the question is, what are each of your businesses or what are you doing in your roles to provide to your customers and to your employees saying, OK, while we are preaching cybersecurity, what are we doing ourselves to make sure that we are not hosting personal information and company information out on the Internet? What are we doing to make sure that our Facebook accounts aren't being seen by everybody? What are you guys doing in order to make sure that you yourselves aren't being socially engineered?

The CHAIRMAN. All right. Anybody want to——

Dr. PAULI. I will jump in there.

The CHAIRMAN. Sure.

Dr. PAULI. I know the university is developing a user-awareness training, which will go out, like every other training, to every faculty, staff, and students.

I am working with organizations. I mentioned Heartland earlier, with Helix Security. That is exactly what they are doing, right? Buzz and everybody at Helix Security is saying, you know, we can develop these models. Russ and his crew at Heartland are pushing those out to their customers.

And user-awareness training and moving along that maturity model is job one, you know. So I think, you know, the university as a whole plays the education role, right? We are educating you and all of your classmates and your colleagues to go out into spots like SBS and Heartland and SDN and everywhere across so that you carry that message forward.

So I hope that the business owners and the business executives back me up on that one.

The CHAIRMAN. Anybody else?

Mr. SHLANTA. You know, from a practice perspective, we have annual training. It is mandatory. At the end of the year, if you are not on the list, we are tracking you down to sit you through training. We will do those trainings on Saturday mornings. We will do those training on Friday evenings for our staff who works weekends and evenings.

In those trainings, we go over, say, network literacy, in terms of just protecting the network, but then also customer information, making sure people understand you can't share customer information. It is just part of the business that we are in. And, if there was a breach, how do you report it, who do you report it to.

So we do that annually. That is one thing we are doing, and I would encourage all businesses to do those things to help educate their employees.

Mr. PULSE. I will jump in. Good question, Tanner. And we use some things similar, as well, from a social engineering perspective. We get phishing e-mails and those sorts of things that are learning tools.

I will tell you, from a social engineering perspective, I had an interesting personal experience where I had just posted a job posting, and I think it might have been 3 days later I got an e-mail to my business e-mail with a resume. It was quarantined because it was infected. I didn't get an opportunity to be dumb enough to open it up, but guess what? I might have. Because I was in that market, right? We had just placed a posting.

So the ingenuity of these people, these attackers, these social engineers, you know, it is crazy. So just being diligent and understanding and knowing that—you know, fortunately, we had some pretty good detective software in place.

Dr. STREFF. Just to add on to that, I mean, I don't think it is enough to——

The CHAIRMAN. Boss?

[Laughter.]

Dr. STREFF. No, I mean, for our customer, I don't think it is enough to just educate them; you have to test them on what they know.

You know, so if you are concerned about phishing in your risk management program, then you have to test to see—you have to train people in phishing, but then you have to test it, right? And 10 times a year, you have to give it to employees and see who is clicking on stuff and see who is not. If you are worried that they are going to hook a USB stick up into your network, then if you are worried about it, then you have to test it.

So, I mean, I think it is one thing to say, you know, have an acceptable use policy, "I will not do that," and it is another thing to train them in that they won't do it, but I think you have to test it. So I think that is the next generation of these services, is to test things out.

65

The CHAIRMAN. OK. Well, that is a really good question, Tanner, and I appreciate you asking it and getting some of the responses to it.

And, you know, we have—and I have seen him in the audience. Nic Budde, who is a DSU grad and does our IT stuff, is constantly harassing people in our office to have strong passwords, among other ways of protecting our information, in addition to some of the things that the Senate already does.

But it is something that I think everybody has to look at a lot more seriously. And we all take a lot of this for granted, but there are lot of bad people out there who want to do bad things. And we just want to make sure that all of you guys out here play for the good side, because we know you are smart enough, probably, to hack into all our computer systems.

Any other questions out there from—yes, sir?

AUDIENCE MEMBER. [inaudible] progress. So how would you go about trying to adjust to that? Because [inaudible]. So my question is, how would you go about that?

The CHAIRMAN. Good question.

Mr. PULSE. I think there is an economic answer to that question, and that is putting pressure on the software vendor. Because, I mean, what else can you do?

You see it every day, where, you know, you have a device that is not patched, but I can't patch that device because I have this piece of software running over here that will break if we do. And the software vendor tells me, "Don't apply that patch."

I think it is an economic thing that we just, collectively—the marketplace needs to correct itself there.

Mr. EPSTEIN. There is a broader question. Those of us who carry Android phones are aware of what is called fragmentation, market fragmentation and update fragmentation.

I happen to—and this is my personal phone, not a government phone—I use Verizon. And this is a Samsung phone. Every time there is a patch released by Google for Android, it has to go from Google to Samsung to Verizon to me. And, historically, each of the intermediary steps have not done a very good job of passing along those patches.

So the vast majority of Android phones out there are unpatched and effectively unpatchable because of the economic incentives, that vendors don't want to risk breaking phones, especially given that phones are replaced very frequently.

So there are economic issues. There are also the social issues of people not wanting to install the patches, either because it is going to break their applications or just because they don't want to take time or they don't want to use data minutes or data megabytes to do the download.

So we have to look at this from a cyber economic perspective, not just a technical perspective. And this is again why we have to look at problems not just as technical problems but as cyber human problems.

The CHAIRMAN. Anyone else?

Yes, sir?

AUDIENCE MEMBER. Yes. So the question was asked earlier, what keeps you up at night and, you know, what scares you in the cyber realm?

I want to tell you, from the perspective of somebody who grew up doing this as a hobby, what scares me is that I, as a security researcher finding problems and then wanting to go and report them, am putting myself in danger. I am walking a thin line between what may be legal and what is not, even if my intentions are good and everything that I am doing is helping.

The Computer Fraud and Abuse Act came in place under the Reagan administration, like, in the 1980s. It is severely outdated. The consensus in the security community is that the law has not kept up with what is going on and that people are afraid to do research and more afraid to tell people about that research once it is done.

So what can we do as a country, as companies, as senators, Congressmen, anything, to let security researchers know that we are behind them and the work that they do is appreciated and helpful?

Mr. STINE. So, when I opened up, I mentioned that NIST is a part of the Department of Commerce. And we have a sister agency, NTIA, that actually has just initiated a multi-stakeholder process looking at things such as vulnerability disclosure in the research community specifically.

So there is a very new opportunity, within the last couple of months, and certainly an ongoing one, to engage in that process as a researcher and then, I think, an interesting perspective as a student, as well, to contribute to that discussion to help us, as Commerce, understand what are the positive research uses for vulnerabilities that are identified, responsible disclosure, those types of things, in the process. And I am happy to share some more information with you out of band.

Dr. PAULI. Andrew, I think what we are going to see is the proliferation of bug bounty programs, right? Some of the companies that are now involved in bug bounties we would have never dreamed were part of bug bounties, right? Bug bounties are the new black, kind of, right now.

So I think we are going to see some spreading of that. I know that doesn't give you the carte blanche that maybe you want, right? It only gives you certain targets. But I think we are going to see a spreading of bug bounties.

The computer abuse and fraud, you are not the first student to bring it up; you won't be the last. I hope we can get some movement on it, as well. But maybe the bug bounties will be a little bit of a pacifier until we get that figured out.

Dr. STREFF. So, Chairman, the story here, then, goes, if somebody finds a flaw, if they report it, they are in trouble, maybe even in jail. And if they give it to a bad guy, they will make money off of that. They can sell it. So it is a double whammy.

The CHAIRMAN. Yep.

Mr. EPSTEIN. So the CFAA, as you say, is one of the areas that researchers point to. The other that is related is the DMCA, the Digital Millennium Copyright Act.

And I do hear this a lot from researchers. Some of the researchers won't tell me what areas they won't research because they are—it is not so much me, but, in general, they don't want to talk about what areas they don't want to research because they are afraid that that might indicate to potential vendors who might want to sue them what areas they think are risky, and so they don't want to tip them off.

So there is no doubt that it is having an impact on the research community because people are afraid to do research. Whether, from a policy perspective, that should be changed or not is a political question, and that is for the senator to decide. But there is no question that it is having an impact on research.

The CHAIRMAN. And I thought I needed a bug bounty in my house.

[Laughter.]

The CHAIRMAN. That is a really good question and, obviously, one that needs to be—it sounds like one that we need to be thinking about, too, in terms of how we support the people who are doing good things out there.

Anything else for the good of the order? Anybody else got a—OK.

AUDIENCE MEMBER. My name is [inaudible]. I am a Cyber Operations Major at Dakota State.

You said earlier what keeps you up at night. What keeps me up at night is [inaudible], not from my wallet, not from a credit card statement [inaudible]. I believe it is a lot easier now to get access to your credit card information through them. And I was just curious to know what is, like, being done about that.

The CHAIRMAN. Does anybody want to take a stab at that?

Dr. PAULI. Anybody from Apple——

[Laughter.]

Dr. PAULI.—on the panel that would care to go on the record?

I think what we are going to have to do is watch and see. There has been no huge, you know, oh, my gosh, you know, Apple Pay is vulnerable to this type of attack. When we see that, and we probably will see that, then we will see some movement from Apple, right? It is the economic ebb and flow of exploitation versus patching.

Should it keep you up at night? I don't know. It might be a worthy reason to keep you up at night. But we haven't seen anything yet; thus, we are not going to see anything from Apple yet. And I know that is very reactionary, but that is the economic reality.

The CHAIRMAN. All right.

Mr. EPSTEIN. I think the bigger risk is not, frankly, to a student who probably doesn't have enough money in your checking account to be worth stealing, if you are anything like I was when I was a student. If I got my account up to $100, I was feeling pretty good.

I think the bigger risk is actually to small businesses. If you as an individual, if there is a theft from your bank account, from your credit card, by and large, banks are either required, if it is a credit card, or voluntarily if it is a debit card, to make you whole again. When it happens to small businesses, when it happens to local governments, it is a lot harder to deal with.

And we know that this happens, and there are, perhaps, regulatory changes but certainly technical changes that we could be doing to encourage small businesses to be using dedicated computers whenever they are processing money instead of using the same computer that they use for other purposes, to be using two-factor authentication with their banks, to prevent malware on their computer from transferring the funds offshore, et cetera.

So there are technical measures that we could be using. There is research to be done, as well. We recently funded a project to look at mobile payment systems that are largely in use in the Third World, where you don't have a credit card and you don't have a bank; you just process the money directly from one phone to another. What are the security risks associated with those? They are in widespread use, especially in Africa and Asia, and nobody knows how bad the security risks are.

So we need to continue research in those areas. And the State Department is cooperating with NSF in that research, with funding the research.

The CHAIRMAN. OK. One more.

AUDIENCE MEMBER. My question is [inaudible]. I want to know what the U.S. knows [inaudible] and what is going to be done.

The CHAIRMAN. Well, that is a good question. I will tell you, what keeps a lot of our military and intelligence community up a lot at night is, you know, what are the rules of engagement in the new world of cyber warfare? And, you know, nation-states, we get hacked, we get attacked; what is a proportionate response?

And so I can tell you that the military and intelligence community are grappling with those types of issues, and I don't know that they have come to any hard and fast conclusions yet.

With regard to law enforcement, on just criminal attacks, I mean, does anybody want to talk about what is being done on that front?

I think it is kind of a whole new world, honestly. But there is going to have to be some consequence and a reckoning for people who steal people's personal information, steal their money by somehow, you know, hacking into their, if it is a phone system or their—I worry about financial services. And everybody does everything online these days, you know. I think there are just all kinds of threats out there and all kinds of risks, and a lot of bad people are trying to exploit it.

I think right now, it seems to me, at least, that most of the prosecution has been case by case and, you know, trying to bring people to justice, but I don't know that there has been a lot of thought given—and I know there is a lot of thought given on the military side to nation-states and, you know, rogue states and terrorist organizations that are trying to hack in and, you know, disrupt some of our critical infrastructure. But on the prosecutorial side, law enforcement side, I am not sure that there is a lot of movement on that front.

And maybe I am—I would look to Nick Rossi, who is a former FBI guy and does a lot of our cybersecurity stuff on the Committee, if you have any thoughts on that.

Mr. ROSSI. Typically, it is a challenge because you have to try to lure folks into a jurisdiction where the U.S. can take custody of them or work out an arrangement with a foreign government in order to follow through on it. And it is a big challenge.

Dr. PAULI. I think on the nation-state side, the writing is on the wall, and it is pretty obviously what we are doing, right?

A couple years ago, we had no Centers of Academic Excellence in cyber operations; now the U.S. has 14. A couple years ago, there was no such thing as U.S. Cyber Command; now we have the U.S. Cyber Command. Six thousand employees in the U.S. Cyber Command, which is the military branch of cyber. The Cyber Command started as this blob of people; now there are 14 very specific job roles within the U.S. Cyber Command.

So, while the Department of Defense probably isn't going to come out and have a press conference and tell us exactly what we are going to do and how we are going to do it and what the thresholds are, I think the writing on the wall is pretty obvious what the Department of Defense is thinking.

Dr. STREFF. I think that is true with offensive capabilities, as well. Businesses can't fight back, right? If we get hacked, if a business gets hacked, you can't just hack back, right? But Cyber Command can.

So that is part of the capability that is being developed there, right? I mean, if you can get somebody to hack them back, then you can get them to maybe stop, and maybe they won't be successful with their attack and you can thwart their attack.

I think there is a lot being done here, but just—you know, law enforcement is understaffed, too, Arnold, right? I mean, you know, FBI has only got so many agents; they can only handle so many cases of certain value in certain jurisdictions. You know, it is an expensive fight.

Dr. PAULI. Yes. And to put a bow on it, maybe it comes full circle. If we are going to do that, right, if we are going to engage U.S. Cyber Command on behalf of Madison Community Hospital, that is going to take information-sharing, which is going to be a heck of a battle coming up, right?

Madison Community Hospital would love that when something happens. "Go get them, go get them, Cyber Command." But that is going to take information-sharing in the good times and in the bad, right? It is a true marriage —good times, bad, health, you know, sickness, all that good stuff.

[Laughter.]

The CHAIRMAN. But if you do visit with our military leadership in the country—and standing up Cyber Command was a really important acknowledgment and recognition, but I think there is still a lot of grappling going on about the, again, proportionate response, rules of engagement.

And, frankly, I am glad, I think we have the most sophisticated operations in the world. And I have visited the NSA facilities up in Maryland and looked at the things that they can do and what the capabilities are, and, you know, we have tremendous capability.

But what are going to be, in this new world—and I think it is a very serious national security consideration and one that is not going away. We are going to be dealing with it well into the future, which is, again, the focus of this hearing and why I appreciate so much our panelists for joining us and all of you for your really good questions.

It is clear that students here at Dakota State University have done their homework. They are asking questions, tough questions, that are hard to answer. But we want to do our best to make sure that we have, as best we can, the answers to those questions for the future.

Because, as I mentioned earlier, by 2020, the estimate is we are going to have 50 billion connected devices in the world. And that creates a tremendous benefit, convenience, opportunity, but also great risk.

And the people who are going to be principally in charge of addressing those risks and trying to prevent those attacks and deal with those are a lot of the folks, hopefully, that are seated in this room. We hope that there are going to be a number of students here at Dakota State University that are going to be leading the way when it comes to helping us deal with these issues in the future.

So I want to thank everybody for attending.

I will say, the hearing record will remain open for 2 weeks, during which time, if there are additional questions that would be submitted for the record, those can be. And, upon receipt, the witnesses are requested to submit their written answers to the Committee for inclusion in the record.

And, with that, we are adjourned. Thank you very much.

[Whereupon, at 4:10 p.m., the hearing was adjourned.]

APPENDIX

Question 1. As attacks and breaches continue to rise, shortages in our cyber workforce need to be addressed. The Cisco Annual Security Report recently stated that the global shortage of cyber professionals is at 1 million openings. Are existing Federal programs like the NIST National Initiative for Cybersecurity Education, the National Cybersecurity Workforce Framework, and NSF's CyberCorps Scholarships steps in the right direction to increase our workforce? What other initiatives do you think would be helpful to build the required workforce—either government initiatives or those by industry or academia?

Answer. The National Science Foundation's (NSF) investments in cybersecurity research are accompanied by investments in cybersecurity education and workforce development. Research undertaken in academia not only engages some of our Nation's best and brightest researchers, but because these researchers are also teachers, new generations of students are exposed to the latest thinking from the people who understand it best. And when these students graduate and move into the workplace, they will bring this knowledge and understanding with them. Moreover, faculty members in this dual role of researchers and teachers have incentives to write textbooks and prepare other teaching materials that allow dissemination of their work to a wide audience, including teachers and students nationwide.

In recent years, the NSF Directorate for Education and Human Resources (EHR) has focused on increasing the number of professionals with degrees in cybersecurity. An overwhelming majority of these EHR-developed professionals were supported by the CyberCorps®: Scholarship for Service (SFS) program.

Through the end of FY 2014, the SFS program has provided scholarships to more than 2,300 students and graduated more than 1,700, including 22 percent with bachelor's degrees, 76 percent with master's degrees, and two percent with doctoral degrees. Of these graduates, 93 percent have been successfully placed in the Federal Government. SFS scholarship recipients have been placed in internships and full-time positions in more than 140 Federal departments, agencies, and branches, and state, local, and tribal governments, including the National Security Agency, Department of Homeland Security, Central Intelligence Agency, and Department of Justice.

NSF believes that basic research in cybersecurity together with research on learning can also address the challenge of expanding existing educational opportunities and resources in cybersecurity. In FY 2014, the Secure and Trustworthy Cyberspace program released a Dear Colleague Letter [1] to encourage new collaborations between the cybersecurity research and computing education research communities. As a result of the Dear Colleague letter, NSF has made 12 cybersecurity education Early Concept Grants for Exploratory Research (EAGER) awards in FY 2015.

NSF is an active participant and contributor in the National Initiative for Cybersecurity Education (NICE) led by the National Institute of Standards and Technology (NIST). The goal of NICE is to establish an operational, sustainable and continually improving cybersecurity education program for the Nation to use sound cyber practices that will enhance the Nation's security. NSF's involvement aims to bolster formal cybersecurity education programs encompassing K–12, higher education, and vocational programs, with a focus on the science, technology, engineering, and mathematics disciplines to provide a pipeline of skilled workers for the private sector and government.

Through NSF's Research Experiences for Undergraduates (REU) program, NSF has supported several REU Sites based on independent proposals that seek to initiate and conduct projects that engage a number of undergraduate students in research. REU Sites must have a well-defined common focus, based in a single dis-

---

[1] *http://www.nsf.gov/pubs/2014/nsf14075/nsf14075.jsp*

cipline or spanning interdisciplinary or multi-disciplinary research opportunities with a coherent intellectual theme, which enables a cohort experience for students. Each REU Site typically supports 8 to 12 undergraduate students each summer, including housing and stipend support, with each student involved in a specific project guided by a faculty mentor. REU Sites are an important means for extending high-quality research environments and mentoring to diverse groups of students. NSF's investments in REU Sites focused on cybersecurity and information assurance include:

- Trustable Computing Systems Security Research and Education at the University of Connecticut;
- Information Assurance and Security at Dakota State University;
- Undergraduates Engaged in Cyber Security Research at the University of Maryland;
- Site for Extensive and Collaborative Undergraduate Research Experience (SECURE) at the University of Nebraska at Omaha;
- Multidisciplinary Information Assurance and Security at Purdue University; and
- Digital Forensics Research in Rhode Island at the University of Rhode Island.

With an emphasis on two-year colleges, the Advanced Technological Education (ATE) program focuses on the education of technicians for the high-technology fields that drive our Nation's economy, including cybersecurity. The program involves partnerships between academic institutions and industry to promote improvement in the education of science and engineering technicians at the undergraduate and secondary school levels. The ATE program supports curriculum development; professional development of college faculty and secondary school teachers; career pathways to two-year colleges from secondary schools and from two-year colleges to four-year institutions; and other activities. Another goal is articulation between two-year and four-year programs for K–12 prospective science, technology, engineering, and mathematics (STEM) teachers who focus on technological education.

The ATE program supports projects, centers, and targeted research on technician education. Activities may have either a national or a regional focus. A project or center is expected to communicate a realistic vision for sustainability and a plan for achievement. It is expected that at least some aspects of both centers and projects will be sustained or institutionalized past the period of award funding. Being sustainable means that a project or center has developed a product or service that the host institution, its partners, and its target audiences want continued.

Of 17 active ATE awards, four are focused on cybersecurity, including a national center, a resource center, and two regional centers:

- National CyberWatch Center (Maryland)—This center, originally established in 2005 at Prince George's Community College and re-funded as a national center in 2012, leads collaborative efforts to increase the quantity and quality of the cybersecurity workforce by advancing cybersecurity education. The center comprises over 50 two-year schools, over 50 four-year institutions in 33 states, over 30 industry partners, three government partners, six public school systems, and two non-profit organizations. It pursues curriculum development, faculty professional development, and K–12 initiatives. It is estimated that over 11,000 students have been impacted by the National CyberWatch Center's faculty development.
- National Resource Center for Systems Security and Information Assurance (CSSIA) (Illinois)—Originally established in 2003, this center, based at Moraine Valley Community College, seeks to support: innovative faculty development; expansion of comprehensive cyber competitions at the higher education and minority levels; development and expansive distribution of high-quality cybersecurity lab content; and remote virtualization content delivery and innovative virtualization lab environments. CSSIA has mentored, established, and expanded cybersecurity degree and certification programs at hundreds of institutions in over 30 states. In 2013 alone, 1,191 students participated in CSSIA-sponsored cybersecurity competitions.
- Cyber Security Education Consortium (CSEC) (Oklahoma)—Based at the University of Tulsa, this center is a partnership of community colleges and career and technology centers in eight states in the central U.S. CSEC has established cybersecurity certificate and degree programs at 49 two-year program sites in eight states, and signed over 120 articulation agreements that provide students with advanced placement, dual enrollment, or cybersecurity course credit at two- and four-year institutions. Since 2004, over 1,300 CSEC students have

completed certificate programs in cybersecurity; over 800 others have received associate degrees; and over 200 others have attained bachelor's degrees in cybersecurity. In the 2013–14 academic year, CSEC had 2,337 security-related student enrollments.

- CyberWatch West (Washington)—The overarching goal of CyberWatch West is to strengthen the cybersecurity workforce in California and the Pacific Northwest. To accomplish this goal, CyberWatch West is concentrating on the following four major areas: (1) student activities, including meaningful internships and a cyber-defense league with weekly virtual exercises; (2) assistance in curriculum development based on recognized standards and creation of cybersecurity pathways from community colleges to four-year institutions; (3) a faculty development and mentor program to help infuse cybersecurity concepts into coursework; (4) outreach and partnership with regional community colleges, universities, high schools, and industry to determine and assist with regional needs in cybersecurity education. CyberWatch West consists of 44 academic partners, plus three high-schools and 19 industry and government partners, and has an active enrollment of nearly 1,000 students, including a large minority student population.

Question 2. The certification organization for cyber professionals, (ISC),[2] recently noted that a poll of 14,000 information security professionals found that only 10 percent were women. In addition to the overall labor shortage in the cyber industry, what can be done to increase representation of women in this particular STEM discipline?

Answer. NSF includes broadening participation in its core values, as it seeks and accommodates "contributions from all sources while reaching out especially to groups that have been underrepresented." This is especially the case within the Computer and Information Science and Engineering (CISE) community, where the longstanding underrepresentation of many demographic groups coincides with the increasingly pervasive role of computing in our society, the importance of IT innovation in driving our economy, and the growing demand for IT specialists at all levels of the workforce. To this end, NSF is working to broaden participation in cybersecurity in a number of ways.

For many kids, the connection between careers and computing is blocked at the high-school level: few of our high-schools teach any computer science (CS). In fact, we teach less computer science in high-school now than we did two decades ago. Only 19 percent of U.S. students take a single CS course. This lack of CS in high-schools disproportionately affects women and minorities: women because they don't see any counters to the popular misconceptions about computing and minorities because they are more likely to attend low-resourced schools that don't offer any CS course.

NSF has funded the development of two new high-school courses: an introductory course called Exploring Computer Science, and a new AP course called CS Principles. Both courses were designed to be engaging and inspiring for all students. Both teach programming but are not programming-centric; rather, they focus on computational concepts, covering the design of algorithms and software, computational problem-solving, the wide range of potentially transformative applications of computing, and ethics and social impacts. These courses are being piloted and adopted in hundreds of schools across the country and many of the pilots are already seeing representative numbers of women and minorities. In addition to a comprehensive CS curriculum, NSF has funded 20 large projects around the country to develop scalable models of teacher professional development.

NSF has also funded the National Center for Women and Information Technology (NCWIT), a non-profit community of more than 600 universities, companies, non-profits, and government organizations nationwide working to increase women's participation in computing and technology. NCWIT equips change leaders with resources for taking action in recruiting, retaining, and advancing women from K–12 and higher education through industry and entrepreneurial careers. NCWIT works to correct the imbalance of gender diversity in technology and computing because gender diversity positively correlates with a larger workforce, better innovation, and increased business performance.

Finally, through the SFS program, NSF has developed and funded the Inspiring the Next Generation of Cyber Stars (or GenCyber) summer camps, to seed the interest of young people, to help them learn about cybersecurity, and to learn how skills in this area could pay off for them in the future. These overnight and day camps are available to students and teachers at the K–12 levels at no expense to them; funding is provided by NSF and the National Security Agency (NSA). A pilot project for cybersecurity summer camps in 2014 stimulated such great interest that the

GenCyber program expanded in 2015, supporting 43 camps held on 29 university campuses in 19 states with more than 1,400 participants (including one GenCyber camp at Dakota State University for girls entering grades 8–12).

Question 3. The Cybersecurity Enhancement Act directed increased coordination on research and development activities across the Federal Government. It also directed activities for research centers, test beds, secure coding, and cloud computing. In your views, what research activities should the private sector, academia, and Federal agencies prioritize? In other words, what do you see as the future of cybersecurity research?

Answer. NSF closely coordinates and collaborates with other Federal agencies and the private sector in pursuing cybersecurity research and development activities. In 2011, the National Science and Technology Council (NSTC), with the cooperation of NSF, put forward a strategic plan titled *Trustworthy Cyberspace: Strategic Plan for the Federal Cybersecurity Research and Development Program.*[2] The Plan specifies four strategic thrusts to organize activities and drive progress in cybersecurity R&D across the Federal Government:

- Inducing Change—Utilizing game-changing themes to direct efforts towards understanding the underlying root causes of known current threats with the goal of disrupting the status quo with radically different approaches to improve the security of the critical cyber systems and infrastructure that serve society.

- Developing Scientific Foundations—Developing an organized, cohesive scientific foundation to the body of knowledge that informs the field of cybersecurity through adoption of a systematic, rigorous, and disciplined scientific approach. Promotes the discovery of laws, hypothesis testing, repeatable experimental designs, standardized data-gathering methods, metrics, common terminology, and critical analysis that engenders reproducible results and rationally based conclusions.

- Maximizing Research Impact—Catalyzing integration across the game-changing R&D themes, cooperation between governmental and private-sector communities, collaboration across international borders, and strengthened linkages to other national priorities, such as health IT and Smart Grid.

- Accelerating Transition to Practice—Focusing efforts to ensure adoption and implementation of the powerful new technologies and strategies that emerge from the research themes, and the activities to build a scientific foundation so as to create measurable improvements in the cybersecurity landscape.

In response to the Cybersecurity Enhancement Act, the Networking and Information Technology Research and Development (NITRD) Cyber Security and Information Assurance Research and Development Senior Steering Group is developing an updated Federal cybersecurity research and development strategic plan. The strategic plan will be used to guide and coordinate federally-funded cybersecurity research.

In August 2015, the President's Council of Advisors on Science and Technology (PCAST) released its review of the NITRD program,[3] which since its establishment in 1991 has coordinated the government's investments in networking and information technology R&D. PCAST noted eight specific areas that are critical to the future of IT, including cybersecurity, and emphasized their relevance to national priorities.

The PCAST report identified Federal investments in at least five key R&D areas that have the potential to improve the foundations of cybersecurity:

- Cybersecurity by Design—An understanding of how to construct secure and trustworthy systems.

- Defense Against Attack—Ongoing mechanisms for authentication, authorization, data provenance, and integrity checks, as well as powerful tools to detect potential vulnerabilities automatically, for systems in use.

- Systems Resilience—Improved methods to mitigate the effects of an attack.

- Implementation Support—Methods to express cybersecurity policies formally in ways that are understandable both to people and to computers and tools to use them for policy implementation and compliance checking.

[2] http://www.whitehouse.gov/sites/default/files/microsites/ostp/fed_cybersecurity_rd_strategic_plan_2011.pdf
[3] https://www.whitehouse.gov/sites/default/files/microsites/ostp/PCAST/nitrd_report_aug_2015.pdf

- Better and faster methods for attribution, enabling both technical and non-technical mitigations.

Question 4. We briefly discussed at the hearing the possible cybersecurity concerns with the proliferation of connected devices and the Internet of Things. Given the wide-ranging applications of cyber-physical systems, many agencies, including the NSF, identify and fund research on such systems. How does NSF work to coordinate that research with other agencies and private sector companies, and what research is NSF currently supporting related to the security of cyber-physical systems?

Answer. NSF coordinates its cybersecurity research and planning activities with other Federal agencies, including the Departments of Defense (DoD) and Homeland Security (DHS) and the agencies of the Intelligence Community, through various "mission-bridging" activities:

- NSF plays a leadership role in the interagency NITRD Program. The National Science and Technology Council's NITRD Subcommittee, which NSF co-chairs, has played a prominent role in the coordination of the Federal Government's cybersecurity research investments.
- In January 2008, President Bush initiated the Comprehensive National Cyber Security Initiative (CNCI).[4] The current Administration supports and has continued efforts on this initiative. One of the goals of the CNCI is to develop "leap-ahead" technologies that would achieve orders-of-magnitude improvements in cybersecurity.
- Based on this directive, a NITRD Senior Steering Group (SSG) for Cyber Security and Information Assurance R&D (CSIA R&D)[5] was established to provide a responsive and robust conduit for cybersecurity R&D information across the policy, fiscal, and research levels of the government. The SSG is composed of senior representatives of agencies with national cybersecurity leadership positions, including: DoD, Office of the Director of National Intelligence (ODNI), DHS, NSA, NSF, NIST, Office of Science and Technology Policy, and Office of Management and Budget. A principal responsibility of the SSG is to define, coordinate, and recommend strategic Federal R&D objectives in cybersecurity, and to communicate research needs and proposed budget priorities to policy makers and budget officials. One of CISE's Division Directors is the co-chair of this group.
- The NITRD Cyber Security and Information Assurance Interagency Working Group (CSIA IWG)[6] coordinates cybersecurity and information assurance research and development across the member agencies, including DoD, the Department of Energy and the National Security Agency, which focus on research and development to prevent, resist, detect, respond to, and/or recover from actions that compromise or threaten to compromise the availability, integrity, orconfidentiality of computer-and network-based systems.

Beyond its coordination with other Federal agencies, NSF also promotes partnerships between academia and industry. These partnerships are critical to a healthy trustworthy computing ecosystem. They enable discoveries to transition out of the lab and into the field as threats and solutions co-evolve over time. And they ensure U.S. leadership, economic growth, and a skilled workforce.

Let's take cyber-physical systems (CPS) as one example. Cyber-physical systems are subject to threats stemming from increasing reliance on computer and communication technologies. Cyber security threats exploit the increased complexity and connectivity of critical infrastructure systems, placing the Nation's security, economy, public safety, and health at risk. NSF is working with its Federal partners (such as DHS, NIST, the Department of Energy, and the Department of Transportation) in many areas of CPS—such as strategic planning of R&D, research collaboration, joint program solicitations, multi-agency proposal review and processing, and co-funding of research proposals.

NSF is also partnering with Intel Corporation in the security and privacy of CPS. The national and economic security of the U.S. depends on the reliable function of critical infrastructure. This infrastructure is rapidly being advanced through the integration of information and communication technologies, leading to cyber-physical systems. Advances in CPS will enable capability, adaptability, scalability, and

---

[4] *http://www.nitrd.gov/subcommittee/csiacyberlink.html*
[5] *https://www.nitrd.gov/nitrdgroups/index.php?title=Cyber_Security_Information_Assurance_Research_and_Development_Senior_Steering_Group_%28CSIA_R%26D_SSG%29*
[6] *https://www.nitrd.gov/nitrdgroups/index.php?title=Cyber_Security_and_Information_Assurance_Interagency_Working_Group_(CSIA_IWG)*

usability that will far exceed the simple embedded systems of today. CPS technologies will transform the way people interact with engineered systems—just as the Internet has transformed the way people interact with information. New smart CPS will drive innovation and competition in sectors such as food and agriculture, energy, different modes of transportation including air and automobiles, building design and automation, healthcare and medical implants, and advanced manufacturing.

The goal of NSF's partnership with Intel is to foster novel, transformative, multidisciplinary approaches that ensure the security of current and emerging cyberphysical systems, taking into consideration the unique challenges present in this environment relative to other domains with cybersecurity concerns. These challenges arise from the non-reversible nature of the interactions of CPS with the physical world; the scale of deployment; the federated nature of numerous infrastructures; the deep embedding and long projected lifetimes of CPS components; the interaction of CPS with users at different scales, degrees of control, and expertise levels; the economic and policy constraints under which such systems must often operate; and the sensing and collection of information related to a large spectrum of everyday human activities. A set of joint NSF/Intel awards was awarded in FY 2015.

A number of NSF-funded researchers, particularly those working in larger, interor multidisciplinary teams, also collaborate closely with industry to deepen and extend the outcomes of their research activities. For example, building on NSF-funded research dating back to FY 2010, researchers at the University of California at San Diego[7] and University of Washington[8] have demonstrated the ability to remotely take over automotive control systems.[9] The researchers found that, because many of today's cars contain cellular connections and Bluetooth wireless technology, it is possible for a hacker working from a remote location to take control of various features—like the car locks and brakes—as well as to track the vehicle's location, eavesdrop on its passenger cabin, and steal vehicle data. The researchers are now working with the automotive industry to develop new methods for assuring the safety and security of on-board electronics. Both the Society for Automotive Engineers (SAE) and the United States Council for Automotive Research (USCAR) have partnered with the researchers to stand up efforts focused on automotive security research.[10] Automotive manufacturers have also started dedicating significant resources to security.[11]

Similarly, NSF-funded researchers at the University of Michigan, University of Massachusetts Amherst, and University of Washington were able to gain wireless access to a combination heart defibrillator and pacemaker, reprogramming it to shut it down and to deliver jolts of electricity that could have potentially been fatal if the device had been implanted in a person. This research team is now collaborating with industry, including the Medical Device Innovation, Safety, and Security (MDISS) Consortium, Association for the Advancement of Medical Instrumentation (AAMI), and specific biomedical device companies, including Medtronic, Philips Healthcare, Siemens Healthcare, and Welch Allyn, to prevent illegal or unauthorized hacking of devices that have wireless capabilities. For each of the last two years, this NSF-funded research team has also held a Medical Device Security Workshop[12] [13] to bring together solution-oriented experts in medical device manufacturing and computer security to meet and discuss effective ways to improve information security and inform Food and Drug Administration (FDA) guidelines on cybersecurity. Additionally, the research team has created a traveling classroom for medical device manufacturers, and has provided private on-site security engineering education and training to over 500 employees from a half-dozen major medical device manufacturers. We expect such academic/industry collaborations to continue to grow as new cybersecurity challenges and results emerge.

[7] http://www.nsf.gov/awardsearch/showAward?AWD_ID=0963702&HistoricalAwards=false
[8] http://nsf.gov/awardsearch/showAward?AWD_ID=0963695&HistoricalAwards=false
[9] http://www.nytimes.com/2011/03/10/business/10hack.html
[10] http://www.autosec.org/faq.html
[11] http://www.caranddriver.com/features/can-your-car-be-hacked-feature
[12] http://secure-medicine.org/workshop/2014
[13] http://secure-medicine.org/workshop/2013

RESPONSE TO WRITTEN QUESTIONS SUBMITTED BY HON. STEVE DAINES TO
JEREMY EPSTEIN

Question 1. Mr. Epstein, you mentioned $158 million was dedicated to cybersecurity research and education in FY 2014, and a portion of this went to prevention and prediction research. Can you elaborate on these preventative measures and how these can help us act proactively instead of reactively?

Answer. The National Science Foundation (NSF) invests in unclassified, fundamental, long-term research in the science of trustworthiness and related trustworthy systems and technologies. The Secure and Trustworthy Cyberspace (SaTC) Program funds research that investigates the motivations and incentives of individuals and institutions, both as attackers and defenders, in order to design and produce software systems that are resistant to attacks by *designing-in security,* to dramatically reduce the number of exploitable flaws.

Today, NSF's cybersecurity research portfolio includes projects addressing security from the microscopic level, detecting whether a silicon chip is a counterfeit or may contain a malicious circuit, to the macroscopic level, determining strategies for securing the next-generation electrical power grid and transportation network, as well as at the human level, studying online privacy and security behaviors of both adolescents and senior citizens, methods for leveraging personality differences to improve security behaviors, and motivations for keeping systems patched.

Examples of research to design-in security includes NSF-funded research dating back to FY 2010, when researchers at the University of California at San Diego [1] and University of Washington [2] demonstrated the ability to remotely take over automotive control systems.[3] The researchers found that, because many of today's cars contain cellular connections and Bluetooth wireless technology, it is possible for a hacker working from a remote location to take control of various features—like the car locks and brakes—as well as to track the vehicle's location, eavesdrop on its passenger cabin, and steal vehicle data. The researchers are now working with the automotive industry to develop new methods for assuring the safety and security of on-board electronics. Both the Society for Automotive Engineers (SAE) and the United States Council for Automotive Research (USCAR) have partnered with the researchers to stand up efforts focused on automotive security research.[4] Automotive manufacturers have also started dedicating significant resources to security.[5]

Similarly, NSF-funded researchers at the University of Michigan, University of Massachusetts Amherst, and University of Washington were able to gain wireless access to a combination heart defibrillator and pacemaker, reprogramming it to shut it down and to deliver jolts of electricity that could have potentially been fatal if the device had been implanted in a person. This research team is now collaborating with industry, including the Medical Device Innovation, Safety, and Security (MDISS) Consortium, Association for the Advancement of Medical Instrumentation (AAMI), and specific biomedical device companies, including Medtronic, Philips Healthcare, Siemens Healthcare, and Welch Allyn, to prevent illegal or unauthorized hacking of devices that have wireless capabilities. For each of the last two years, this NSF-funded research team has also held a Medical Device Security Workshop [6] [7] to bring together solution-oriented experts in medical device manufacturing and computer security to meet and discuss effective ways to improve information security and inform Food and Drug Administration (FDA) guidelines on cybersecurity. Additionally, the research team has created a traveling classroom for medical device manufacturers, and has provided private on-site security engineering education and training to over 500 employees from a half-dozen major medical device manufacturers. We expect such academic/industry collaborations to continue to grow as new cybersecurity challenges and results emerge.

Question 2. Mr. Epstein, in your testimony, you talked about a cybersecurity expert shortage. Can you explain how cybersecurity presents an opportunity for high tech jobs in all areas of the U.S.?

Answer. With the rapid pace of technological advancement, daily life is now intimately connected to the Internet. Key aspects of business operations, our financial systems, manufacturing supply chains, and military communications are tightly networked, integrating the economic, political, and social fabric of our global society.

---

[1] http://www.nsf.gov/awardsearch/showAward?AWD_ID=0963702&HistoricalAwards=false
[2] http://nsf.gov/awardsearch/showAward?AWD_ID=0963695&HistoricalAwards=false
[3] http://www.nytimes.com/2011/03/10/business/10hack.html
[4] http://www.autosec.org/faq.html
[5] http://www.caranddriver.com/features/can-your-car-be-hacked-feature
[6] http://secure-medicine.org/workshop/2014
[7] http://secure-medicine.org/workshop/2013

These interdependencies can lead to vulnerabilities and a wide range of threats that challenge the security, reliability, availability, and overall trustworthiness of all systems and resources rooted in information technology. Due to the fast growth of the cybersecurity field, the Nation is facing a scarce talent pool, with thousands of positions to fill as demand for a well-trained cybersecurity workforce continues to rise. The U.S. Bureau of Labor Statistics expects employment of information security analysts to grow by 37 percent by 2022, a rate far greater than the average growth rate for all other jobs.[8]

To address the important issues in the preparation of tomorrow's cybersecurity workforce, NSF's investments in cybersecurity research are accompanied by investments in cybersecurity education and workforce development in order to inform and grow a prepared U.S. workforce with the competencies essential to success in an increasingly competitive global market.

In recent years, NSF has focused on increasing the number of professionals with degrees in cybersecurity. An overwhelming majority of these professionals were supported by the CyberCorps®: Scholarship for Service (SFS) program. The SFS program provides scholarships to students who in turn work for the federal, state, local, or tribal government or related organizations after graduating. The program is offered at 55 college and universities, with additional participating institutions added every year. Through the end of FY 2014, the SFS program has provided scholarships to more than 2,300 students and graduated more than 1,700, including 22 percent with bachelor's degrees, 76 percent with master's degrees, and two percent with doctoral degrees. Of these graduates, 93 percent have been successfully placed in the Federal Government. SFS scholarship recipients have been placed in internships and full-time positions in more than 140 Federal departments, agencies, and branches, and state, local, and tribal governments, including the National Security Agency, Department of Homeland Security, Central Intelligence Agency, and Department of Justice.

NSF is also an active participant and contributor in the National Initiative for Cybersecurity Education (NICE) led by the National Institute of Standards and Technology. The goal of NICE is to establish an operational, sustainable and continually improving cybersecurity education program for the Nation to use sound cyber practices that will enhance the Nation's security. NSF's involvement aims to bolster formal cybersecurity education programs encompassing K–12, higher education, and vocational programs, with a focus on the science, technology, engineering, and mathematics disciplines to provide a pipeline of skilled workers for the private sector and government.

The Advanced Technological Education (ATE) program focuses on the education of technicians, for the high-technology fields that drive our Nation's economy, including cybersecurity. The program involves partnerships between academic institutions and industry to promote improvement in the education of science and engineering technicians at the undergraduate and secondary school levels. The ATE program supports curriculum development with an emphasis on two-year colleges; professional development of college faculty and secondary school teachers; career pathways to two-year colleges from secondary schools and from two-year colleges to four-year institutions; and other activities. Another goal is articulation between two-year and four-year programs for K–12 prospective science, technology, engineering, and mathematics (STEM) teachers who focus on technological education.

Question 3. Mr. Epstein, in the research that the NSF has completed on cybersecurity, have you seen any trends in the source of attacks? Are most threats domestic or international? Are the international threats concentrated in certain regions or countries?

Answer. NSF does not directly research or assess the source of cyberattacks on the United States. However, NSF closely collaborates with other Federal mission-agencies on cybersecurity. For example, NSF co-chairs the Networking and Information Technology Research and Development Program (NITRD) Cyber Security and Information Assurance (CSIA) Senior Steering Group (SSG), which provides leadership across the government in cybersecurity research and development by serving as a forum for information sharing and cross-agency agency setting. The SSG is composed of senior representatives of agencies with national cybersecurity leadership positions, including: the Department of Defense, the Office of the Director of National Intelligence, the Department of Homeland Security, the National Security Agency, the National Institute of Standards and Technology, the Office of Science and Technology Policy, and the Office of Management and Budget. A principal re-

---

[8] *http://www.bls.gov/ooh/computer-and-information-technology/information-security-analysts.htm*

sponsibility of the SSG is to define, coordinate, and recommend strategic Federal R&D objectives in cybersecurity, and to communicate research needs and proposed budget priorities to policy makers and budget officials.

———

RESPONSE TO WRITTEN QUESTIONS SUBMITTED BY HON. JOHN THUNE TO KEVIN STINE

Question 1. As attacks and breaches continue to rise, shortages in our cyber workforce need to be addressed. The Cisco Annual Security Report recently stated that the global shortage of cyber professionals is at 1 million openings. Are existing Federal programs like the NIST National Initiative for Cybersecurity Education, the National Cybersecurity Workforce Framework, and NSF's CyberCorps Scholarships steps in the right direction to increase our workforce? What other initiatives do you think would be helpful to build the required workforce—either government initiatives or those by industry or academia?

Answer. The National Initiative for Cybersecurity Education (NICE), led by NIST, with support from other Federal agencies including the Office of Personnel Management (OPM), the Department of Defense (DoD), and the Department of Homeland Security (DHS), is working with government, academia, and industry to establish a new strategic plan as called for in the Cybersecurity Enhancement Act. Under NIST leadership, the strategic plan anticipates building on existing successful programs, instituting new creative approaches, and instilling a spirit of continuous improvement designed to increase impact as measured by appropriate metrics of effectiveness. The new strategic plan also calls for the acceleration of learning and skills development to create a sense of urgency for closing the talent gap. NICE has increased its investment and emphasis on industry engagement to discover and highlight effective practices and solutions that are being deployed to train, or retrain the existing workforce.

As part of their support for the NICE program, DHS led development of the National Cybersecurity Workforce Framework (Workforce Framework). The Federal Government, educational institutions, and several industry sectors are implementing the Workforce Framework, and we believe that greater use of the Workforce Framework will lead to improved talent management. We believe that NICE is building momentum that will enable its partners—both in government and industry—to increase the availability of a qualified cybersecurity workforce.

Question 2. The certification organization for cyber professionals, (ISC)², recently noted that a poll of 14,000 information security professionals found that only 10 percent were women. In addition to the overall labor shortage in the cyber industry, what can be done to increase representation of women in this particular STEM discipline?

Answer. NIST is currently leading development of a new strategic plan for the NICE program. This new strategic plan will include an objective to encourage creative and effective efforts to increase the number of underrepresented populations, including women, minorities, and veterans. NICE is also committed to creating a culture of evidence that uses data to analyze current workforce data and project future trends.

There are numerous initiatives in place across the country to increase the number of women in cybersecurity that NICE intends to support. For example, several of the GenCyber Camps (*http://www.gen-cyber.com/*) funded by NSA and NSF are focused on increasing girls' interest in cybersecurity careers. There is also a growing network of women who serve as mentors, including the annual Women in Cybersecurity Conference (*https://www.csc.tntech.edu/wicys/*) funded by the National Science Foundation. Additionally, DHS is a sponsor of the Air Force Association's CyberPatriot program. CyberPatriot's goals include promoting STEM and cyber education among young women. Through partnerships such as these, the NIST NICE program office and NICE partner agencies are working to mentor girls and young women with the goal of inspiring them to pursue STEM and cybersecurity professions.

NICE anticipates the facilitation of a workshop in 2016 that will inventory and analyze existing programs, and develop a Call for Action that identifies a strategy and path forward for increasing the representation of women in cybersecurity.

Question 3. The Cybersecurity Enhancement Act directed increased coordination on research and development activities across the Federal Government. It also directed activities for research centers, test beds, secure coding, and cloud computing. In your views, what research activities should the private sector, academia, and Federal agencies prioritize? In other words, what do you see as the future of cybersecurity research?

80

Answer. NIST is committed to the value of communicating its cybersecurity research and development (R&D) efforts to industry, academic, and government colleagues and identifying opportunities to collaborate and support R&D efforts across these communities. NIST is one of several Federal agencies working together through the Networking and Information Technology Research and Development (NITRD) Program to provide a framework in which many Federal agencies come together to coordinate their networking, IT, and cybersecurity R&D efforts.

Under this program, agencies are collaborating to develop the Cybersecurity Research and Development Strategic Plan called for in the Cybersecurity Enhancement Act. The new plan aims to identify research opportunities intended to thwart adversaries, expand trust, and sustain innovation, focusing on desired cybersecurity capabilities that deter attackers, protect assets, detect attacks, and respond using effective mitigation, forensics, and adaptive defense techniques. Cross cutting issues will also be explored such as the human centric nature of cybersecurity, risk management, scientific foundations, infrastructure/data development/access, transition to practice, and workforce development. Additionally, it will consider emerging technologies and expanding threats in relation to mobile, cloud, IoT/CPS, additive manufacturing, and pervasive use of cryptography.

Question 4. We've heard very positive feedback about the NIST Framework for Improving Critical Infrastructure Cybersecurity. Some of the cited benefits of the Framework include the creation of a common language and greater involvement of company executives in cybersecurity decision making. What steps has NIST taken to ensure industry is aware of the Framework and is using it to the fullest extent? What does NIST plan to do to keep it up to date?

Answer. Since the release of the Framework, NIST has strengthened its collaborations with critical infrastructure owners and operators, industry leaders, government partners, and other stakeholders to raise awareness about the Framework, encourage use by organizations across and supporting the critical infrastructure, and develop implementation guides and resources.

NIST supports Framework awareness and understanding by addressing a variety of sectors and communities through speaking engagements and meetings. NIST develops and disseminates information and training materials that advance use of the Framework, including actual or exemplary illustrations of how organizations of varying sizes, types, and cybersecurity capabilities can practically employ the Framework to make their enterprises more secure.

NIST provides an *Industry Resources* page on its Cybersecurity Framework website (*http://www.nist.gov/cyberframework/cybersecurity-framework-industry-resources.cfm*). This page provides publicly available Framework resources produced by critical infrastructure owners and operators, industry associations, technology manufacturers and service providers, government agencies, and others. These resources include, but are not limited to approaches, methodologies, implementation guides, mappings to the Framework, case studies, foreign language translations and other materials intended to help organizations understand, use, and innovate on the Cybersecurity Framework to identify, assess, and manage cybersecurity risk.

The Framework is a living document and will continue to be updated and improved as industry provides feedback on implementation. Lessons learned will be integrated into future versions of the Framework. NIST plans to issue a Request for Information in the fall of 2015 to obtain additional input from industry on the variety of ways in which the Framework is being used to improve cybersecurity risk management, how best practices for using the Framework are being shared, the relative value of different parts of the Framework, the possible need for an update of the Framework, and options for the long-term governance of Framework.

Question 5. A number of Federal agencies have issued guidance that incorporates or implements the NIST Cybersecurity Framework for different critical infrastructure sectors. Which agencies has NIST been working with most closely? How do those agencies ensure the Framework does not conflict with existing standards in those sectors?

Answer. NIST has worked with numerous Federal agencies to assist with the implementation of the NIST Cybersecurity Framework across industry. This includes regular participation in workshops and events hosted by other agencies, including those run by the Department of Homeland Security. NIST has also assisted in guidance done collaboratively with industry, such as the Energy Sector Cybersecurity Framework Implementation Guidance and the Federal Communications Commission (FCC) Communications, Security, Reliability and Interoperability Council's (CSRIC) *Cybersecurity Risk Management and Best Practices Working Group 4: Final Report.* During the development of the Cybersecurity Framework, considerable attention was spent ensuring alignment with existing standards. Since the issuance of the Framework, NIST continues to provide advice to agencies, sectors, associations, and other groups to ensure proper alignment.

Question 6. Federal agencies have suffered numerous cyber attacks this past year, including high-profile incidents at OPM, IRS, the Pentagon, and the White House. While some Federal agencies have made improvements to their cybersecurity practices, weaknesses still remain. Are there lessons from the private sector or academia that can be applied to the government? What steps has NIST taken recently to address identified vulnerabilities at Federal agencies as part of its work under the Federal Information Security Management Act (FISMA)?

Answer. NIST routinely collaborates with nonfederal organizations in the development of its security standards and guidelines. In addition to direct interactions with industry and academic institutions, nonfederal organizations frequently provide important feedback to NIST during the public comment period of the standards and guidelines development process. This helps to ensure that leading-edge cybersecurity concepts, principles, and solutions are incorporated into NIST's publications (for example, NIST Special Publication 800–53 Rev 4, *Security and Privacy Controls for Federal Information Systems and Organizations*). As part of its significant outreach program, NIST visits Federal agencies on a regular basis to discuss ongoing cybersecurity issues and problems. This includes examining specific vulnerabilities that may have been exploited during a cyberattack or other events that lead to a cyber breach or compromise of Federal information. NIST uses this information to assess the completeness and efficacy of the current security safeguards and countermeasures that are included in the suite of Federal standards and guidelines and to ensure the appropriate defensive measures are available to Federal agencies. These collaborative outreach activities have been increased due to the recent cyberattacks and the severity of the breaches.

Question 7. The National Security Agency Information Assurance Directorate recently announced it will "initiate a transition to quantum resistant algorithms in the not too distant future." Since NIST specified the Suite B cryptographic algorithms, how is NIST engaging academia, industry, standards setting bodies, and its Federal partners in order to research and identify quantum resistant algorithms in a transparent and open manner?

Answer. NIST initiated its Quantum Resistant Algorithms program on April 1–2, 2015 with an open and transparent public *Workshop on Cybersecurity in a Post-Quantum World.* At this workshop, NIST engaged industry, academia, Federal partners and other stakeholders to understand and discuss requirements, threat models, and priorities in quantum resistant algorithm research, development and standardization.

In FY16, NIST intends to finalize its initial requirements and scope of work, seeking broad community input and feedback through participation in public industry events and in open standards bodies. Additionally, NIST actively solicits public engagement and feedback on all cryptographic standards and guidelines through our public comment process, which is described in NIST Draft Interagency Report 7977, *NIST Cryptographic Standards and Guidelines Development Process.*

RESPONSE TO WRITTEN QUESTIONS SUBMITTED BY HON. STEVE DAINES TO KEVIN STINE

Question 1. Mr. Stine, the NIST cybersecurity framework seems to be focused on businesses. What framework or guidance applies to schools? Has NIST dedicated any resources specifically to student data privacy?

Answer. The NIST Cybersecurity Framework, while developed for critical infrastructure, is also available for use by other types of organizations, including non-profit organizations and educational institutions. For example, the "Information Security Guide" (*http://educause.edu/security/guide*) maintained by EDUCAUSE, a non-profit association of colleges and universities, is organized according to the ISO 27002 standards, but includes a mapping to the NIST Cybersecurity Framework.

Student data privacy is not a specifically addressed by NIST, although the Cybersecurity Framework provides the guidance by which an educational institution can protect information, including student educational records and personally identifiable information. Student data privacy is addressed in the Federal Government by the U.S. Department of Education.

Question 2. Mr. Stine, we heard from the other witnesses how businesses are working every day to ensure their customers privacy and personal information remains secure. Is the government taking these same precautions to protect the per-

82

sonal information of American citizens? Can you explain what steps the government takes to deal with cyber threats and cyber terrorists?

Answer. Like businesses, the government faces cybersecurity challenges. NIST develops and issues standards, guidelines, and best practices to help Federal agencies manage cybersecurity risk and protect mission information, including the personal information of American citizens, from a variety of cyber threats, including those posed by cyber terrorists. The development of NIST standards and guidelines includes a comprehensive, collaborative, and transparent public consulting process that invites and incorporates input and comments from government, industry, and academia. This process ensures that the security standards and guidelines developed by NIST for Federal agencies and their contractors are timely, effective, rigorous, comprehensive, and reflective of security best practices employed by industry, academia, and government. The sharing of best practices and lessons learned between and across government and the private sector will benefit all. While NIST does not have an operational role in responding to cyber threats or cyber terrorists, NIST supports other agencies, including the Department of Homeland Security, in ways that are consistent with its mission.

Question 3. Mr. Stine, through the OPM breach, we learned that the Federal Government's National Cybersecurity and Protection System (NCPS) is not keeping pace with the types of threats now facing Federal agencies. What steps can the government take today to prevent another OPM breach?

Answer. Questions related to the National Cybersecurity Protection System (NCPS) should be directed to the Department of Homeland Security as they have responsibility for this program.

NIST develops standards, guidelines, measurements, tools and reference implementations that Federal agencies can use to identify, assess, and manage cybersecurity risk. The Federal Information Security Modernization Act of 2014 (FISMA 2014) reaffirmed NIST's role of developing Federal information processing standards (FIPS) and guidelines for non-national security Federal information systems and assigned NIST some specific responsibilities, including the development of:

- Standards to be used by Federal agencies to categorize information and information systems based on the objectives of providing appropriate levels of information security according to a range of risk levels;
- Guidelines recommending the types of information and information systems to be included in each category; and
- Minimum information security requirements (management, operational, and technical security controls) for information and information systems in each such category.

A key aspect of a risk management approach to cybersecurity is an organization's informed selection and implementation of the appropriate set of security and privacy controls to provide adequate protection for Federal information and information systems. Properly applied in a comprehensive approach to cybersecurity, the controls can help significantly reduce susceptibility of Federal agencies to modern cyber threats. This application requires employing a risk-based, defense-in-depth strategy that includes strengthening the underlying IT infrastructure to increase the penetration resistance of Federal information systems to cyber-attacks; designing security architectures that help limit the damage to Federal assets if an adversary successfully penetrates those systems; and making the systems sufficiently resilient to survive the attack and continue to operate and support critical Federal missions and business functions. While no security control or group of controls can stop every attack, implementing a risk-based, defense-in-depth strategy greatly reduces the susceptibility of Federal agencies to modern cyber threats.

RESPONSE TO WRITTEN QUESTIONS SUBMITTED BY HON. JOHN THUNE TO MARK SHLANTA

Question 1. As attacks and breaches continue to rise, shortages in our cyber workforce need to be addressed. The Cisco Annual Security Report recently stated that the global shortage of cyber professionals is at 1 million openings. Are existing Federal programs like the NIST National Initiative for Cybersecurity Education, the National Cybersecurity Workforce Framework, and NSF's CyberCorps Scholarships steps in the right direction to increase our workforce? What other initiatives do you think would be helpful to build the required workforce—either government initiatives or those by industry or academia?

Answer. Addressing shortages in our country's cyber workforce is an important national priority. SDN Communications, like many business organizations and the Federal Government, relies upon skilled cybersecurity professionals, but experiences difficulty when recruiting these workers. There is competition between the private and government sectors to recruit the limited pipeline of high-skilled cybersecurity professionals graduating from academic institutions, like Dakota State University (DSU). The Federal Government should maintain its support for programs, like the National Institute for Standards and Technology (NIST) National Initiative for Cybersecurity Education, the National Cybersecurity Workforce Framework, and the National Science Foundation's CyberCorps Scholarships, to increase this critical workforce.

SDN has partnered with DSU and the Federal Government to support cybersecurity camps. The camps sponsored by the National Security Agency and National Science Foundation are an effective tool to inspire and educate young people about opportunities within cybersecurity fields. The Federal Government and higher education institutions should maintain their support for these educational initiatives and partner with private industry to extend the reach of these valuable programs.

Given the competition for skilled cybersecurity professionals and challenge recruiting these workers, companies should focus on growing their workforce from within by providing training and educational benefits. SDN provides internship opportunities to post-secondary students as an investment in the next crop of cybersecurity professionals. The internship program also helps the company recruit future employees. SDN's people are the company's most valuable asset. Through tuition benefits and other internal and external training opportunities, SDN is continually strengthening the skills of its workforce. It is essential that we make smart investments in our employees to ensure our company can continue combating rapidly evolving and sophisticated cybersecurity threats.

Question 2. The certification organization for cyber professionals, (ISC)², recently noted that a poll of 14,000 information security professionals found that only 10 percent were women. In addition to the overall labor shortage in the cyber industry, what can be done to increase representation of women in this particular STEM discipline?

Answer. With the shortage of cybersecurity professionals reaching an astonishing 1 million, addressing the labor shortage will require not only greater female representation in cybersecurity careers, but also outreach to other underrepresented populations. According to a report from the American Association of University Women (AAUW), one in five male college students and only one in 17 female college students plan to major in engineering or computing. The study found there is a similar retention rate for both men and women, 60 percent in engineering and 40 percent in computing. The AAUW report highlights the importance of generating interest in cybersecurity career fields at an early age to influence a student's academic field of study and future career aspirations.

As mentioned in the response to question one, SDN has partnered with the Federal Government and higher education to support cybersecurity camps. Last summer, SDN served as the leading private sponsor of the Girls GenCyber Camp held on the DSU campus. The camp, one of the first in the nation, narrowed its eligibility to young women between the ages of 12 to 18 years old and encouraged the participants to pursue cybersecurity careers. When the 60 available spots quickly filled, SDN sponsored 40 additional young women. The Federal Government, higher education, and private industry should build upon the successful experiment launched at DSU to help address the insufficient pipeline of female cybersecurity professionals.

Question 3. The Cybersecurity Enhancement Act directed increased coordination on research and development activities across the Federal Government. It also directed activities for research centers, test beds, secure coding, and cloud computing. In your views, what research activities should the private sector, academia, and Federal agencies prioritize? In other words, what do you see as the future of cybersecurity research?

Answer. As discussed during the field hearing on September 3, 2015, cybersecurity threats are a significant and growing concern facing the Federal Government and every industry sector. Cybersecurity research represents a worthwhile investment in bolstering our country's ability to address these threats. Recognizing the importance of cybersecurity research and development, Congress should prioritize strong and continued funding for the research activities outlined in the Cybersecurity Enhancement Act.

The Federal Government should encourage collaboration between its academic and private research partners. Greater collaboration between the Federal Government, critical infrastructure operators, and academia could be helpful in identifying valuable research topics. The Federal Government can maximize the effectiveness of its research investments by directing funding toward research projects aimed at addressing our country's leading cybersecurity challenges.

Outreach and the sharing of research findings is another important priority. Those receiving Federal research funding should be encouraged to consider effective ways to share their discoveries. Expanding the adoption of best practices and proven techniques can help organizations reduce their risk of cyber breaches and improve their ability to detect and respond in the event of cybersecurity attacks.

Question 4. Federal agencies have suffered numerous cyber attacks this past year, including high-profile incidents at OPM, IRS, the Pentagon, and the White House. While some Federal agencies have made improvements to their cybersecurity practices, weaknesses still remain. Are there lessons from the private sector or academia that can be applied to the government?

Answer. The recent series of cyber attacks exposed weaknesses in the Federal Government's preparedness against cybersecurity threats. In the case of the U.S. Office of Personnel Management, the absence of basic security precautions, such as two-step authentication, exposed the agency to heightened vulnerability that was exploited by hackers. Consistent adoption and enforcement of best practices and internal security controls would reduce risk and improve the Federal Government's ability to detect and respond to cyber threats.

As described in the written testimony prepared, SDN Communications enforces an internal cybersecurity program. The Federal Government should ensure similar controls and policies are implemented. A general description of some of the security protocols followed by SDN is outlined below. This represents a limited sample of the procedures SDN uses to protect its internal business network.

SDN protects its network with an enterprise firewall that enforces rules and only accepts traffic from approved external IP addresses. The company conducts daily and sometimes hourly antivirus definition updates to improve the detection of malicious software and prevent harmful downloads. Regular patches to SDN's operating system, PCs, and other devises close security gaps that could be exploited. Any patch deemed critical to protecting SDN's equipment and servers is performed immediately.

The company enforces access policies that require passwords to be regularly changed and pin codes and badges in order to enter physical locations. Virtual and physical locations are limited to the employees who require access in order to perform their job responsibilities. Cameras and door access logs are equipped throughout the company premise, and fingerprint entry is required at SDN's most secure locations. SDN requires employees working remotely to utilize an SSL Virtual Private Network (VPN) and perform two-factor authentication to access the company's network. This encryption service masks all traffic between SDN's network and the end user.

The company's local administrator policy and account usage monitoring prevents unsanctioned software downloads onto company-issued equipment. Limiting an employee's ability to download malicious software helps reduce the risk of social engineering attacks. SDN also blocks foreign devices from accessing its network using a Network Access Control (NAC) appliance to prevent unauthorized devices from connecting to the network. Outside laptops and mobile devices cannot connect to the company's private Wi-Fi network and are segregated onto a guest Wi-Fi network.

The NIST Framework established a common language to encourage greater collaboration across the Federal Government and industry sectors. The utilization of the NIST Framework by the Federal Government and operators of critical infrastructure can help to facilitate the sharing of best practices and adoption of effective cybersecurity techniques. The NIST Framework can equip Federal agencies, as well as the private sector, with a useful tool to critically evaluate and further strengthen cybersecurity programs.

The risk of reputational harm, liability, and other costs associated with cybersecurity breaches have prompted many businesses—both large and small—to make significant investments in their cybersecurity programs. In the case of SDN, our organization is continually making investments to further protect its network and the sensitive information we have been entrusted. In applying this lesson to the Federal Government, agency budget requests should reflect the importance of cybersecurity network maintenance and improvements. Boards of directors and executive leadership in the private sector are increasingly demanding that cybersecurity be a top organizational priority. When confirming agency officials, the U.S. Senate should

85

similarly demand that appointees to Federal agencies recognize the importance of cybersecurity.

———

RESPONSE TO WRITTEN QUESTIONS SUBMITTED BY HON. STEVE DAINES TO MARK SHLANTA

Question 1. Mr. Shlanta, your company participates in the NIST cybersecurity framework. Does this framework provide adequate guidance to help you protect your customers? In what areas does industry need additional guidance or legislation to help sector secure our information?

Answer. The National Institute for Standards and Technology (NIST) Framework serves as a useful tool to assist organizations in examining their cybersecurity practices. SDN Communications is a business-to-business broadband provider and offers a variety of cybersecurity services to its customers, including Managed Router, Managed Firewall, Managed Distributed Denial of Service (DDoS) Protection, Remote Network Monitoring, and Secure Data Storage. The company serves as a cybersecurity partner to numerous critical infrastructure sectors.

The creation of a common language regarding cybersecurity, extending across industry sectors, is one of the benefits that emerged from the NIST Framework. This common language encourages improved understanding and collaboration between critical infrastructure operators and the government as they work together to address cybersecurity threats.

The value of the NIST Framework stems from its voluntary, flexible, and scalable nature. Its flexibility enables the guidance to evolve with changes in technologies, cybersecurity threats, and the unique needs of critical infrastructure operators utilizing the framework. The NIST Framework helps shift our national focus from a "check-the-box" mentality towards a risk-based approach tailored to addressing and mitigating unique organizational risk.[1] This is more effective than strict and prescriptive regulation that would struggle to keep up with emerging and constantly evolving threats. According to Booz Allen Hamilton's "2014 Cyber Solutions Handbook," cybersecurity is intimately tied to an organization's unique operations, and therefore, companies must assess their unique organizational risk when designing and maintaining their cybersecurity programs.[2]

Although the NIST Framework is based upon existing regulatory standards and industry best practices, the framework itself is still relatively new. The guidance from the Federal Communications Commission's Communications Security, Reliability, and Interoperability Council (CSRIC) was released in March 2015, giving communications providers less than a year to review and utilize these recommendations relating to the NIST Framework. The CSRIC guidance included a useful section tailored to small and mid-size communications carriers.[3] It will take time for small operators to learn about, digest, and apply the NIST Framework and CSRIC guidance to their existing cybersecurity programs. Some small operators may even need one-on-one technical assistance. As such, congressional policymakers and Federal agencies should focus on raising awareness and making training and other educational resources available to encourage further utilization of the NIST Framework.

As a company, SDN is working with our national and state industry trade associations to raise awareness about the NIST Framework and serve as a useful resource to smaller operators. Topics relating to the NIST Framework and cybersecurity have been on the agenda at every national meeting since the framework's release in February 2014. NIST and its Federal agency partners should build upon these industry efforts and continue working to raise awareness and provide consultative assistance by expanding their outreach activities, including in rural areas. These outreach efforts would expedite the utilization of the NIST Framework by helping providers apply the guidance to their unique operations.

Question 2. Mr. Shlanta, in your testimony, you gave a real example of a cyber threat via social media. When SDN becomes aware of these threats what steps do you take to prepare, prevent, and combat these attacks?

———

[1] "Cyber Solutions Handbook," Booz Allen Hamilton, 2014, page 4, retrieved from *http://www.boozallen.com/content/dam/boozallen/documents/Cyber-Solutions-Handbook.pdf.*
[2] *Ibidem.*
[3] "Cybersecurity Risk Management and Best Practices," Working Group 4, Communications Security, Reliability, and Interoperability Council, Federal Communications Commission, 2014, page 370, retrieved from *https://transition.fcc.gov/pshs/advisory/csric4/CSRIC_IV_WG4_Final_Report_031815.pdf.*

Answer. The attack described in my testimony featured a distributed denial of service (DDoS) attack targeting the domain names of the State of South Dakota and the City of Sioux Falls. DDoS attacks have become increasingly prevalent and pose a growing threat to organizations relying upon the Internet to conduct their business and operations. Preparing for these attacks is an important component of cybersecurity risk management. A DDoS protection service can equip an organization with the necessary tools to prepare, prevent, and combat DDoS attacks.

DDoS attacks disable an online service by overwhelming a targeted IP address with massive data traffic. As a result, an attack can interrupt an organization's website, customer orders, and even phone systems by preventing the flow of legitimate traffic to the targeted network. These attacks can be purchased for as little as $5 per hour, making them an affordable and highly accessible attack platform for cyber criminals, cyber activists, unscrupulous businesses competitors, disgruntled former employees, or dissatisfied customers.[4] The frequency of DDoS attacks has grown, with attack incidents doubling between the second quarter of 2014 and the second quarter of 2015.[5] Given the growing number of attacks and consequences to targeted organizations, it is important for organizations to take proactive steps to protect their networks against these threats.

In October 2015, SDN Communications added a Managed DDoS Protection service to its menu of cybersecurity solutions. *Figure 1* demonstrates the DDoS attack structure, and *Figure 2* shows how SDN's Managed DDoS Protection service detects and prevents the flow of malicious traffic, represented by a red arrow, while allowing the delivery of legitimate traffic, represented by a green arrow. This service is constantly evolving to respond to changing DDoS attack profiles. Known attack signatures from around the world are used to inform the identification of suspicious traffic patterns. When SDN's cybersecurity team detects a new threat, our team works to quickly stop the threat before it impacts our customer, and the attack signature is shared with our security partner Arbor Networks. The product is then updated to identify future attacks bearing the signature.

Figure 1. DDoS Attack Structure [6]

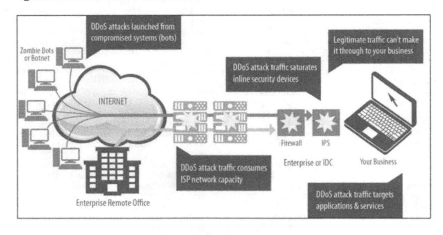

[4] "Global Security Report," Trustwave Holdings, 2015, page 48, retrieved from: *https://www2.trustwave.com/rs/815-RFM-693/images/2015_TrustwaveGlobalSecurityReport.pdf.*

[5] "State of the Internet Security Q2 2015 Report," Akamai, 2015, page 5, retrieved from: *https://www.stateoftheinternet.com/downloads/pdfs/2015-cloud-security-report-q2.pdf.*

[6] "DDoS Attack Structure," SDN Communications, 2015.

Figure 2. DDOS Mitigation Solution [7]

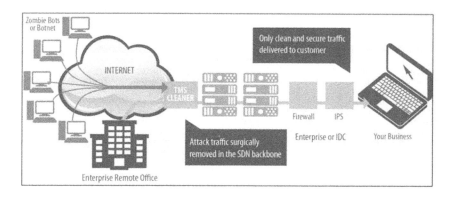

TMS Cleaner - Device that cleans the traffic

ISP - Internet Service Provider

IPS - Intrusion Protection System

IDC - Internet Data Center

RESPONSE TO WRITTEN QUESTIONS SUBMITTED BY HON. JOHN THUNE TO
ERIC A. PULSE

Question 1. As attacks and breaches continue to rise, shortages in our cyber workforce need to be addressed. The Cisco Annual Security Report recently stated that the global shortage of cyber professionals is at 1 million openings. Are existing Federal programs like the NIST National Initiative for Cybersecurity Education, the National Cybersecurity Workforce Framework, and NSF's CyberCorps Scholarships steps in the right direction to increase our workforce? What other initiatives do you think would be helpful to build the required workforce—either government initiatives or those by industry or academia?

Answer. I believe the existing Federal programs mentioned are an excellent start. I believe two points deserve attention: ensuring this information is shared and communicated between public and private sectors, and further integration into academia. Emphasis on cybersecurity at early stages of education could prove beneficial to the needed growth in the cyber workforce. Integrating basic cybersecurity concepts at grade and middle school levels would build a foundation on which to spur interest at an early age.

I believe there is also an opportunity for organizations to work together to identify specific cybersecurity workforce needs and collaboratively provide a platform to develop a workforce with necessary skills training to fill those needs.

Question 2. The certification organization for cyber professionals, (ISC)², recently noted that a poll of 14,000 information security professionals found that only 10 percent were women. In addition to the overall labor shortage in the cyber industry, what can be done to increase representation of women in this particular STEM discipline?

Answer. As stated earlier, I believe placing emphasis on cybersecurity at early stages of education could prove beneficial to the needed growth in the cyber workforce. Integrating basic cybersecurity concepts at grade and middle school levels would build a foundation on which to spur interest at an early age. The earlier females are introduced to the field, the more likely the increase in overall participation. I also believe that creating mentorship programs that encourage women already in the security field to mentor other women in the technology field positively impact female involvement in cybersecurity.

---

[7] "DDoS Mitigation Solution," SDN Communications, 2015.

Question 3. The Cybersecurity Enhancement Act directed increased coordination on research and development activities across the Federal Government. It also directed activities for research centers, test beds, secure coding, and cloud computing. In your views, what research activities should the private sector, academia, and Federal agencies prioritize? In other words, what do you see as the future of cybersecurity research?

Answer. Threat intelligence collaboration. With cyber threats on the rise, I believe in the collaboration of public and private resources to share information about the attacks that are on the horizon. Cybersecurity by its nature is more reactive than proactive. Perpetrators are able to advance their tactics more rapidly than the defensive infrastructure. The "Deep Net" contains a number of forums offering free attack tools available to anyone with the goal of initiating any number of attack scenarios. An attacker can launch an attack at any time toward any target and the use of botnets make tracing the attack extremely difficult. The commercialization of malware tools also allows the hacking community to remain a step ahead. However, the more a specific type of attack occurs, the better the chance of recognizing it by collaboratively sharing threat intelligence. Network defense and incident response require a strong element of intelligence and counterintelligence that security teams must understand and leverage to successfully defend their cyber infrastructure, once again highlighting the need for an increase in technically qualified professionals.

Question 4. Federal agencies have suffered numerous cyber attacks this past year, including high-profile incidents at OPM, IRS, the Pentagon, and the White House. While some Federal agencies have made improvements to their cybersecurity practices, weaknesses still remain. Are there lessons from the private sector or academia that can be applied to the government?

Answer. Accountability. In the private sector, much of the regulatory guidance emphasizes executive and board involvement relative to overall responsibility for securing information and the infrastructure that supports it. Organizations in the private sector are required to report breaches in order to meet regulatory compliance. Corporate officers and boards of directors are also held accountable for their actions or in-actions. I believe government should enforce the same reporting requirements and implement a culture of accountability to be more responsible to the people— ours is a government of, by and for the people. One state government (Oklahoma) has an initiative to consolidate its cybersecurity efforts and to better manage the public resources it receives. This initiative has had some early successes and by all indicators will continue.

RESPONSE TO WRITTEN QUESTIONS SUBMITTED BY HON. JOHN THUNE TO
DR. KEVIN F. STREFF

Question 1. As attacks and breaches continue to rise, shortages in our cyber workforce need to be addressed. The Cisco Annual Security Report recently stated that the global shortage of cyber professionals is at 1 million openings. Are existing Federal programs like the NIST National Initiative for Cybersecurity Education, the National Cybersecurity Workforce Framework, and NSF's CyberCorps Scholarships steps in the right direction to increase our workforce? What other initiatives do you think would be helpful to build the required workforce—either government initiatives or those by industry or academia? SBIR programs could encourage ideas/inventions focused on this unique problem.

Answer. Without question, the NIST National Initiative for Cybersecurity Education, the National Cybersecurity Workforce Framework, and NSF's CyberCorps Scholarships steps in the right direction to increase our workforce. However, this massive projected shortage will not be filled with these three important initiatives. Industry sponsored initiatives will become important to build out this workforce. For example, SFS–I (scholarship for service—industry) could be created to model the SFS program so that industry attracts more cybersecurity professionals. Industry sponsored hacking competitions where industry professionals square off can also garner a lot of attention and serve to attract workforce.

Question 2. The certification organization for cyber professionals, (ISC)², recently noted that a poll of 14,000 information security professionals found that only 10 percent were women. In addition to the overall labor shortage in the cyber industry, what can be done to increase representation of women in this particular STEM discipline?

Answer. Dakota State boasts the largest cyber girls camp in the Nation. With this foundation, DSU can do more to work with other universities to replicate our model. For example, GenCyber attracted 150 girls for a one-week summer camp to introduce them to cybersecurity. This model (marketing, materials, etc.) can be leveraged in other community colleges and universities to attract more women. Retooling programs/grants should be considered to retrain female IT professionals into the cybersecurity domain. SBIR programs could encourage ideas/inventions focused on this unique problem.

Question 3. The Cybersecurity Enhancement Act directed increased coordination on research and development activities across the Federal Government. It also directed activities for research centers, test beds, secure coding, and cloud computing. In your views, what research activities should the private sector, academia, and Federal agencies prioritize? In other words, what do you see as the future of cybersecurity research?

Answer. This research agenda will change each year, so identifying the top areas of research for today seems pointless. Rather, the Federal Government should identify a group responsible for establishing the research agenda and work with academia and industry to make progress. The lack of a fresh national cybersecurity strategy highlights this shortcoming.

Question 4. The Federal Financial Institutions Examination Council recently came out with a tool for financial institutions that maps guidance to the NIST Framework for Improving Critical Infrastructure Cybersecurity. Given your work with small and medium-sized enterprises, how do we get small businesses to appreciate cyber risks, while ensuring that guidance isn't one-sized fits all?

Answer. The Federal Financial Institutions Examination Council cybersecurity assessment "tool" isn't really a tool, but rather guidance on how to assess cyber risk in the banking sector. It also doesn't address how we get small businesses to appreciate and/or deal with their cyber exposures. Clear guidance on specific steps small businesses must take is needed. For example, all business are required to carry E&O insurance. Should all businesses be required to run antivirus? Without very clear requirements, small businesses will likely remain on the sideline and their businesses will remain vulnerable.

Question 5. Federal agencies have suffered numerous cyber-attacks this past year, including high-profile incidents at OPM, IRS, the Pentagon, and the White House. While some Federal agencies have made improvements to their cybersecurity practices, weaknesses still remain. Are there lessons from the private sector or academia that can be applied to the government?

Answer. Information sharing between academia, government and industry is paramount. The three parties must share information, tools, best practices, etc. if we are to mature our defense capabilities. Making the ISACs free for everyone is a good first step. Charging membership fees is a bad idea and will not result in everyone participating as is necessary for an information sharing model to work. The result will likely be that the large organizations will participate and the medium and small sized organizations will not.

Question 6. Thank you for the opportunity to hold this field hearing at Dakota State University. What do you envision DSU's role in advancing cybersecurity will be in five or ten years and how does that vision complement efforts to improve cybersecurity across the nation?

Answer. Dakota State currently enrolls approximately 600 students in its security program. We envision this doubling or tripling over the next 10 years. We anticipate research programs that focus on specific areas in which DSU has excellence, including network testing, offensive tools, and securing the financial sector. Everyone must do more to create tools, workforce and a shared mindset to build our capabilities in the area of cyber defense. Thank you for the opportunity to participate in this hearing.

———

RESPONSE TO WRITTEN QUESTION SUBMITTED BY HON. STEVE DAINES TO DR. KEVIN F. STREFF

Question. Dr. Streff, you mentioned in your testimony that America's national cybersecurity strategy was last updated in 2003. Can you explain the importance of a national strategy in enabling the U.S. to better prevent cyber attacks?

Answer. The strategy is important for several reasons. First, it serves to bring awareness to this national issue. It serves to build agreement on what the issue is and what is necessary to deal with it effectively. Next, it serves as the backdrop for which other strategies, grant programs, etc. fit. For example, if information sharing is an important aspect of dealing with the cyber adversary, then the national strategy should highlight its role and industry, government and academia should work to execute the concept. Grant programs (*i.e.,* SBIR programs, NSF programs, etc.) can pick up on the important aspects of the strategy and allocate dollars accordingly. Industry can also invest in solutions with confidence that there will be a market for their products and services.

Security is a complicated issue and how our Nation goes about its approach is complicated. Many strategies are possible and each include assumptions. These assumptions and strategies should be debated so that an approach is devised. This approach should be documented and disseminated so that all parties understand what it will take in this electronic battle.

On a personal note I remember getting a new President at our university who didn't really understand security. When America's National Strategy to Secure Cyberspace was drafted, it indicated to him how important this issue might become and supported me in getting resources to create a security program. Today I am proud to boast that Dakota State has one of the top programs in the country, and the 2003 document had something to do with where we are today.

Thank you for the opportunity to address the importance of freshening or rewriting our national cybersecurity strategy.

––––––––

RESPONSE TO WRITTEN QUESTIONS SUBMITTED BY HON. JOHN THUNE TO
JOSH J. PAULI, PH.D.

Question 1. As attacks and breaches continue to rise, shortages in our cyber workforce need to be addressed. The Cisco Annual Security Report recently stated that the global shortage of cyber professionals is at 1 million openings. Are existing Federal programs like the NIST National Initiative for Cybersecurity Education, the National Cybersecurity Workforce Framework, and NSF's CyberCorps Scholarships steps in the right direction to increase our workforce? What other initiatives do you think would be helpful to build the required workforce—either government initiatives or those by industry or academia?

Answer. NSF's CyberCorps program is a tremendous asset to the cybersecurity workforce shortage at the government level. It does need to be expanded as we aren't even keeping up with demand currently, let alone filling the empty positions. NSF also partnered with NSA on the GenCyber Camps, which provide cybersecurity content to high school students and teachers. This is another good way to get additional future employees interested in the field. Other agencies need to develop and fund CyberCorps-like programs to attract students into jobs. Such a program could offer a subset of the benefits of CyberCorps and still attract tremendous talent. We also need to reach down deeper into middle and high schools to recruit students into cybersecurity programs.

I strongly encourage NIST to take on a more active role within the cybersecurity workforce efforts in the same way DHS, NSA, and NSF have. The NIST NICE and National Cybersecurity Workforce Framework are great resources that need to be implemented by a wider audience. NICE should be the entity that truly leads the charge for cybersecurity education and workforce development by partnering with NSF, NSA, and DHS (and others certainly) to come up with agile strategies to help develop courses, programs, and graduates that are cyber-ready. This is not trivial work. This is an issue we've been battling for 10+ years, but we have to keep working on it. We need to come up with new ideas and try these ideas in a real-world setting to see if they work.

We need to continue and hopefully expand "special hiring authority" and "direct hiring authority" programs that allow Federal offices to quicken the hiring process for cybersecurity professionals. We can't do too much about the pay, but people want to work at the Federal level for the mission above pay. So let's make it as streamlined as possible to get these people placed. This is 100 percent applicable at almost every Federal agency.

Not enough government entities ever engage the true hacker and professional cybersecurity communities. Cybersecurity is a huge industry by itself, but it's also present in every single other industry. These people want to help the government figure out hard problems because it would make everyone's life better. They are wildly smart and creative. They think of things that government-only efforts just can't or don't. We need to engage these people to inject new ideas and to leverage them as magnificent thinkers in ways to come up with workforce development ideas.

Question 2. The certification organization for cyber professionals, (ISC)², recently noted that a poll of 14,000 information security professionals found that only 10 percent were women. In addition to the overall labor shortage in the cyber industry, what can be done to increase representation of women in this particular STEM discipline?

Answer. Summer camps such as GenCyber, especially those that partner with existing female groups such as the Girls Scouts' GenCyber camp in San Bernardino, CA and the GenCyber Girls camp at Dakota State University, should continue to stress the tremendous job prospects in cybersecurity industry for females. Including computer science and programming requirements in the high school curriculum would also provide additional exposure of cybersecurity foundations to female students. Once female students are fully engaged with cyber, they realize a very high percentage of job satisfaction. The challenge is to reach female students early enough before they have already discounted cyber as a field of study and career path. Efforts such as *Code.org* and Microsoft's TEALS (*https://www.tealsk12 .org/*) should be implemented in all 50 states to better prepare all students for STEM careers.

Question 3. The Cybersecurity Enhancement Act directed increased coordination on research and development activities across the Federal Government. It also directed activities for research centers, test beds, secure coding, and cloud computing. In your views, what research activities should the private sector, academia, and Federal agencies prioritize? In other words, what do you see as the future of cybersecurity research?

Answer. There are so many domains within cybersecurity that have limitless research potential in the near future, but I will list just a few that I believe are the most critical. First, the widespread adoption of user-friendly encryption techniques for all data (at rest and in transit) will continue to be an important research topic. We simply need to get to a place where all data is encrypted in a strong manner and have it implemented for all users.

Next, secure software engineering should continue to be explored as an answer to the on-going software vulnerability epidemic. This goes beyond secure programming concepts, and also includes protocols (a new version of HTTPS is needed that includes security from the planning phase forward) and distributed environments (cloud computing) that are so pervasive now.

Lastly and perhaps most importantly, an intersection of policy and technical solutions is needed to clearly articulate the USA's position on cyber operations. There are many levels to this decision and capability: military, government, private industry, and civilians are a general list of actors that need a clear "rules of engagement" for cyber operations. As a nation, we need to continue to develop our cyber capabilities as the cyber domain continues to become an ever bigger factor in global relations and conflicts. This ties directly into the information sharing efforts between and among government and private entities.

Question 4. Federal agencies have suffered numerous cyber attacks this past year, including high-profile incidents at OPM, IRS, the Pentagon, and the White House. While some Federal agencies have made improvements to their cybersecurity practices, weaknesses still remain. Are there lessons from the private sector or academia that can be applied to the government?

Answer. The private sector has many aspects that government can learn from. Some will argue that regulation is the key to strong cybersecurity, but I am against that thinking. Regulation has a role in the overall cybersecurity levels of an organization, but it should be in place to provide best practices and minimum standards. Very few companies that are only compliant are also secure. Being secure includes many more facets than compliance alone. Additionally, and more importantly, compliance does not fully cover all the facets that make a company secure. Private companies have made the investment in people and technology that directly impact the security of their environments. This is true of regulated environments and unregulated environments alike.

Academia has a very poor cybersecurity posture right now, which makes them the #3 target of hackers right now only behind government and healthcare. Academia has no standards or regulation related to cybersecurity in addition to the "free thinking" aspects of higher education that make implementing a cybersecurity strategy a tough challenge, so it is not a good situation currently in academia. We have a lot to learn and implement to get to where we need to be as an industry given the sensitive data that we house.

Question 5. Thank you for the opportunity to hold this field hearing at Dakota State University. What do you envision DSU's role in advancing cybersecurity will be in five or ten years and how does that vision complement efforts to improve cybersecurity across the nation?

Answer. I believe DSU will play a prominent role in cybersecurity research and development (R&D) with Federal Government agencies such as the National Security Agency (NSA), Department of Defense (DoD), National Science Foundation (NSF) and other like-minded agencies. We have refined our academic programs for

92

the past five years and we are now in a position to conduct applied research in these same areas of cyber operations, secure software engineering, and network security. DSU will continue our role as one of the most prominent cybersecurity institutions, at all academic levels, in the Nation and a place that government and private firms can come to for world-class cybersecurity interns and career placements.

———

RESPONSE TO WRITTEN QUESTION SUBMITTED BY HON. STEVE DAINES TO JOSH J. PAULI, PH.D.

Question. Dr. Pauli, you talked about the need for a higher quantity and quality of graduates to meet the growing demand for cybersecurity and how changes in K–12 can attract more students to this field. But attracting more students into programs doesn't guarantee quality. What programs and policies does Dakota State University utilize to guarantee that program graduates are equipped with the skills needed to enter the workforce?

Answer. DSU, as an institution, has an open enrollment policy so we do not limit the quantity of students attending the university. Thus, we are left to ensure quality is ensured at the program level. We do this by a couple of approaches. We take very seriously the academic rigor of our courses. We are constantly evaluating not only the content of the coursework, but also are instructional methodologies and student engagement techniques. Our BS in Cyber Operations curriculum is mapped directly to the knowledge units as mandated by the National Security Agency as one of 14 Centers of Academic Excellence in Cyber Operations. Our other academic programs are part of our institution-wide designation from NSA and DHS as a Center of Academic Excellence in Information Assurance Education. We also take very seriously the program and student assessments mechanisms that we use during the exit exams as each student graduates the program. Lastly, we stay very closely connected to all of our employers, both in the government and private sector, to ensure DSU graduates are adequately prepared to excel in an internship and full-time career setting.

○

This page intentionally left blank.

94

This page intentionally left blank.

This page intentionally left blank.